All rights reserved.

Copyright © 2024 Mercy .J Simon

Simple Techniques for Successful Mini Farming

Mercy .J Simon

Simple Techniques for Successful Mini Farming : Maximize Your Mini Farm Yield with Easy Methods and Proven Strategies

Funny helpful tips:

Stay connected with your business community; networking offers growth opportunities.

Rotate between books that challenge and comfort; while some stimulate growth, others offer solace.

<u>Life advices:</u>

Engage with virtual reality; its immersive experiences are transforming gaming, education, and training simulations.

Rotate between structured and free reading; while curriculums offer direction, spontaneous choices spark joy.

Introduction

This book provides a comprehensive guide to building a successful mini farm, covering everything from business planning to practical farming techniques.

The guide begins with an exploration of the components of a business plan, including an analysis of past performance, an overview of the current situation, and a SWOT analysis. It emphasizes the importance of setting objectives, key strategies, sales forecasts, and action plans.

The basics of mini farming are then detailed, covering soil health management, preparing soil for planting, creating raised beds, and dealing with pests and diseases. The guide also explores various aspects of mini farming, such as raised bed gardening, prevention of pests and diseases, seed starting, and raising chickens for eggs and meat.

Readers are guided through the process of starting a mini farm, from family groupings to dealing with pests and diseases, raising chickens, and processing meat chickens. The guide also provides tips on harvesting, preserving, and getting the most out of various vegetables.

A section on tools and techniques covers essential aspects such as planting guides, seeders, heated water platforms, plant support, and weed control. The guide concludes with a focus on achieving greater food self-sufficiency through making country wines, vinegar, and cheese at home.

Overall, this book serves as a valuable resource for those looking to embark on mini farming, offering practical insights and step-by-step guidance at every stage of the process.

Contents

PART I: BUILD A PLAN 1
Components of a Business Plan: A RoadMap to Success 2
Overview of Current Situation 7
Altering Your Business Plan 18
PART II: BASICS OF MINI FARMING 20
Managing Soil Health: Concepts and Practices 22
Creating a Raised Bed 28
Prevention is Better Than Cure: Dealing With Pests and Diseases 33
Seed Starting 40
Guide to Growing Fruit Trees and Vines 42
Raising Chickens for Eggs 45
Raising Chickens for Meat 50
Too Much Harvest, Not Enough Time 56
PART III: GETTING THE MOST OUT OF YOUR VEGGIES 59
Soil and Fertility 59
Asparagus 64
Beets and Chard 70
Cabbage, Broccoli, and Cauliflower 77
Corn 82
Potatoes 89
Peppers 94
Onions 99
Turnips, Rutabagas and Radishes 103
Carrots and Parsnips 109

Tomatoes. 114
Beans. 120
Cucumbers. 125
Greens 130
Herbs..136
PART IV: TOOLS AND TECHNIQUES...141
Planting Guides and Seeders 142
Heated Water Platform 146
Support Your Plants...148
Winning the Battle of the Weeds. 151
PART V: GREATER FOOD SELF-SUFFICIENCY. 154
Making Your Own Country Wines. 156
Making Your Own Vinegar. 168
Making Cheese at Home. 174
CONCLUSION. 177

PART I: BUILD A PLAN

Long before the first seed is planted and the cool earth turned to create the furrow, a farmer conceives the idea to produce a crop and make something edible from the land. This annual act of turning the soil and planting the seed, so commonplace to those of us who know agriculture, is in fact something of a miracle. Every spring, the earth renews itself, and those involved in gleaning the goods of Mother Nature's bounty play a role in this eternal cycle.

Very few people now ever get to know the daily joys and trials of building their lives from the land and homes where they live. Today, farmers make up roughly two per cent of the population of the United States. The agrarian way of life is being replaced by new technology, industrialization, and sheer economies of scale. Fortunately, small farmers, or those who desire to be small farmers, have many chances at success. There are opportunities in the marketplace to remain viable and thrive, and these opportunities don't require becoming enormous to survive the commodity-market system. But you need to do more than buy a few cows or plant some soybeans and field corn. To be a successful small farmer, you must have a measure of ingenuity, a surplus of determination, the understanding of a targeted niche market, and, frankly, a high tolerance for the trial and error of entrepreneurship. If you're serious about building a company, changing your destiny, and making a living from home, your first step is drafting a business plan.

You may think you don't need a business plan if you're not ready to get started or if you're unsure if your idea will even work. Farmers tend to be doers, however, not planners. We're often the type who rises early and works hard, being task-oriented and not feeling satisfied until the job at hand is done. These are wonderful qualities, but sometimes we might not see the forest for the trees. In my view, an orderly business plan and the discipline to execute it are essential tools for success with a small-farm venture.

The more organised you are from the start, the better. A formal business plan will help you streamline and solidify your ideas; clearly visualize what works and what doesn't; organize your ideas from the start to ensure a solid approach; and gather financing from lenders or private investors.

Components of a Business Plan: A Road Map to Success

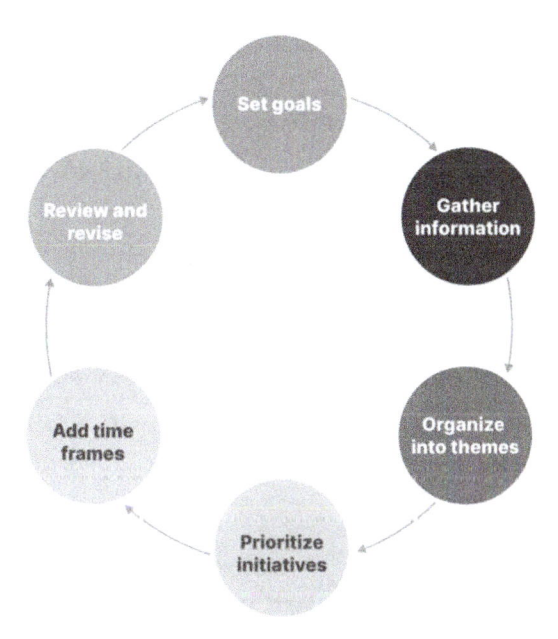

Key components in and organisation's success will depend on a great degree on how well you;
- can gather and interpret information
- adapt to change
- manage staff and resources
- promote your business
- look after customers and more.
- This is where forward planning can help you.

A colleague once told me that 'even a bad plan is better than no plan at all'. A bad plan at least shows that you have given some thought to the direction you want to go in.

A good plan takes time and effort, especially the first time you do one and many business owners or operators think they don't have the time, or don't see the value in it. But believe me... it is worth the time and effort!

It is an opportunity for you to build solid foundations for your small farm, based on known facts and these allow you to:
- be very accurate in your plans and future projections.
- avoid unforeseen pitfalls and crisis situations
- spend your money and/or other resources in the most effective way
- stay ahead of the market
- make the most of every opportunity
- be pro active and choose your own course rather than be reactive and follow everyone else
- stop wasting time, effort and resources on inefficient processes and more

Good business planning involves:
- looking at what you've done in the past few years
- looking at where you are now
- drawing conclusions from the above two points
- based on that information determining your objective for the coming year/s
- setting key strategies to help achieve the objective

Analysis of Past Performance

In this section of a business plan you look at the past year (or two) to take a good look at what worked and what didn't. Where you came from is every bit as important as where you are going. You need to look at:

What promotional activities did you run – for example did you have any discount deals, special offers etc?
- What worked? What didn't?
- Why did the activities work so well, not so well – find the reasons
- Advertising campaigns
- (again) What worked? What didn't?

- Why did the campaigns work so well, not so well - find the reasons
- What mediums did you use? (ie Newspapers, magazines, radio. List the actual companies you used as you may have used a number of different ones.)
- How much did you spend on them?
- Which ones generated enquiries and which ones didn't?
- Did you keep track of the enquiries, if so, what were the results?

Keeping statistics on where enquiries come from can help you to use your advertising budget in the most effective way. There's no point in spending a lot of money on advertising on television, for example, if most of your enquiries come from newspaper ads or word of mouth. Asking customers where they heard about you and keeping a record is the best way of determining advertising effectiveness.

Were there any noticeable or unusual increases or decreases in your business? If so, why did they happen?

Were the increases/decreases at any particular time of the year, or did they affect any particular product or service. If so why? Do a detailed analysis of product and service sales. How many of each individual product or service did you sell? Break these figures up by month as this will, again, show up regular high and low periods which will then allow you to forward plan. For example in high sales periods you know that you will have to order more stock and put on more staff whereas in low demand periods you order less. You can plan for these peaks and troughs in advance... because you have statistically shown that they are coming.

Did your competitors do anything that impacted on your business? If so, what was it?

- How did it affect you?
- Are they likely to do it again?
- What did you (or could you) do about it?

- Budgets – Income and expenses. This is extremely important and we will look at this in detail later in the document. Over the years these statistics will build an extremely accurate picture of your expenditure habits and sales that will show trends. With this information you can anticipate what is going to happen and proactively avoid any pitfalls or take advantage of upcoming opportunities. You can forecast - with a fairly high degree of accuracy - how much you will earn and spend in the coming year. While you might have an accountant to look after the "book keeping" for you, it is essential that you know exactly where your money is being spent and what your income is made up of.

The answers to these and any other questions relevant to your particular industry and business will give you a solid base upon which to build your plans for the future. Knowing how you got to where you are now can show you where you went right... and where you went wrong and gives a clear

Conclusions

Looking at the above information - what conclusions can you draw? For example:
- What will you do again next year and why?
- What won't you do again next year and why?
- What will you do differently and why?
- Were there any lessons to be learned?
- What were they?
- Did you spend money on areas that were unsuccessful / unsuccessful?
- How much?
- Was this money well spent? Why / why not?
- Which products sold well / not well?
- Will you expand your product line?
- Are there any products you should discontinue?

Overview of Current Situation

It is very important to have a firm grasp of your current business environment. This is where you look at what is happening around you right now. Things that are happening that could potentially have an impact on your business. This will:

- give you a clear idea of any issues that might get in the way of your plans in the foreseeable future
- give you the opportunity and the time to take proactive action on any of these issues. This is much better than having to "react" to a change or problem that you didn't anticipate.

It's like having a high powered torch in a tunnel as opposed to a match!

A good overview of your current situation will involve looking at:
- the business environment in which you are operating
- your strong and weak points
- what your competitors are doing.

Business Environment Analysis

What exactly does "business environment" mean?

At its widest view point it can mean the sum total of a number of external and internal factors that affect you and the organisation you work for.

External factors could include such things as:
- **Political issues.** The stability of the Government can have a dramatic affect on the country's or state's economy.
- **Legislative issues.** New legislation can have an impact on your particular industry.
- **Economic Trends.** Are people spending money? What are they spending it on and so forth.
- **Social Trends.** What's in.. what's not? Safety & security issues as well as environmental protection issues etc are

considered here.
- **Competitors.** What is your competition doing and how does that affect your business?
- **Technology.** This is an area that is constantly changing and can have quite an impact on the way business is done.

Also known as a PLESCT Analysis this is a thorough look at the world around you and the influences various issues may have upon your customers, suppliers and therefore your business. Doing this type of research means that you should not be caught unawares by new legislation, trends, changes or advancements. PLESCT stands for: Political, Legislative, Economic, Social, Competitor and Technology and looks at each of these sectors and how they may affect you positively - or negatively .

Doing a PLESCT Analysis

Some of the issues to consider when doing this analysis can include such things as:
- Political issues. Here you should look at the general political stability of the country or state.
- Is there an election due? People get nervous around election times and are cautious about spending / investing their money
- Has there just been an election? In which case is the new government likely to make changes to the status quo - and if so, how will this affect you?
- International economic and social environment – how stable is the situation?

and so on....

For example changes in government often have an impact on businesses dealing with health, education and employment as existing programs are often changed or discontinued after an election, or new programs are introduced. International economic crises often have a big impact on our own market as does the increasing threat of terrorism or conflict situations.

Legislative issues

Have any new legislations been passed / or amended that affect your industry?

If so, what will you have to do to comply with them? How will these changes affect:
- staff?
- resources?
- policies and procedures?
- costs?
- Do you need to obtain any licenses or permits?

Economic issues and trends
- What is the current economic climate?
- Does the current international climate have an effect on us?
- Are people spending more / less money?
- What are they spending it on?
- Are they likely to spend it on your product or service?

For example, the cost of living is currently rising faster than wages - things such as petrol prices and interest rates are increasing rapidly and people are thinking twice about spending their hard earned money.

Social issues and trends
- People will often be influenced in their purchase decisions by "what's IN", or may wish to keep pace with friends

- Environmental issues such as water saving, conserving energy and so on can have an impact on people's purchasing decisions and so need to be considered
- Cultural issues also need to be considered - people from different countries and backgrounds have views and customs that may dictate how they make their purchasing decisions.

Competitor information – This is a very important part of your business environment analysis – you need to know as much as you can about your competitors. Questions you need to ask are:
- Who are they?
- Where are they located?
- How big are they (compared to you)?
- Do they have any affiliations?
- What are their promotional activities?
- How do they advertise?
- What do they advertise?
- How does their product range compare to yours?
- How do their prices compare to yours?
- How does their service compare to yours?
- What impact do they have on your business?

The answers to these questions will give you an overview of how you compare to them and what you can do to improve, and therefore win extra business.

If practical, a product/price comparison grid is an excellent way of keeping an eye on how you are faring against them.

It's also a good idea to also do a SWOT Analysis on your main competitors (next section) - you need to be able to:
- counter their strengths
- take advantage of their weaknesses
- take advantage of the same opportunities and
- maximise their threats.

Technology -
- Is there any new technology available that will have an impact on the way you do business?
- Is it viable for you to adopt this new technology from a cost point of view?
- Can you afford not to adopt this new technology from an efficiency point of view?
- What impact does the internet and electronic means of communication have on your business?

Internal influences also need to be taken into considerations and could include:
- The overall economic state of your business. Is it doing well or not?
- Change of ownership or management of the business. This could have a big affect on the internal workings of the company and the company morale.
- Change of direction for the business. Are you offering new services or products?
- Updating or upgrading of the business. New premises, new equipment etc.
- Down or Upsizing. Are you laying off staff or hiring more?

Looking at the PLESCT Analysis and your internal influences in detail will give you a firm understanding of what is going on around you, and will help you:
- avoid unpleasant surprises that could be costly and damaging to your business
- stay a step ahead of your competitors
- help you take advantage of new opportunities quickly
- minimise the impact of negative trends.....

SWOT Analysis

A SWOT analysis allows you to have a deep down, honest look at your organisation in terms of its strengths, weaknesses, opportunities and threats and to look at ways to make you stronger.

Strengths

What are your organisations strong points? For example:
- Do you have a great location?
- Is it easily accessible?
- Is it a long established company?
- Does it have an excellent reputation?
- Does if offer anything unique?
- Do you have a lot of repeat business?
- Are your prices the best?
- Are you a market leader?

and so on.

Weaknesses

What are your organisations weaknesses? For example:
- Is it a newly established business and not yet well known
- Is the infrastructure in the surrounding area poor making it difficult for customers to get to you?
- Are there any problems with suppliers or staff?

and so on. A point to remember is that not all weaknesses are negative and could be viewed as opportunities for improvement.

Opportunities

What opportunities are there that you could take advantage of? For example:
- New legislation opening new markets to you
- New housing or business developments bringing new customers into your area
- New technology that will make your production or processes more efficient

- Introduction of new product or service lines that will increase revenue

and so on.

Threats
- What things could stop you from achieving your goals? For example:
- A new competitor in the marketplace
- A change in legislation that will mean major changes to your business practices.
- Re-zoning of your area or roadways changing and taking customers away from their current routes (where you are located)

and so on.

Conclusion:
- When looking at your SWOT Analysis what areas need to be addressed?
- Strengths – what can you do to capitalise or maximise on them?
- Weaknesses – what can you do to minimise or negate their impact. Which of them can be turned around to become a strength?
- Opportunities – what do you need to do to take advantage of these opportunities? How can you ensure you get your slice of this opportunity?
- Threats – what can you do to avoid or minimise the impact of the threat?

The answers to these questions will form part of your business plan.

Objective for Next Year

Having looked at your past analysis and current business situation you should now have a solid grasp of your business and where it needs to go to remain successful. Your endeavours to date will now give you a clear direction - or objectives - to aim for in the next one to three years.

One overall objective will have a number of Key Strategies - each of which will, in turn, have a set of tactics designed to help achieve each strategy and therefore the ultimate goal.

- Your objective is WHERE you want to be in a given period of time (ideally 1 - 3 years)
- Your Key Strategies are WHAT you need to do to achieve the objective and
- Your Tactics are HOW you are going to go about actually making it work

Key Strategies

The objective, as stated, is where you want to be. The key strategies are the issues you need to address in order to achieve the objective; WHAT needs to happen. For example if your objective is to increase your revenue by 10% over the previous year, then typical key strategies could be:

- Introduce a new product range to fill an identified market need
- Decrease expenditure by 15%
- Increase your customer base by 10%

All of which would work towards achieving the overall objective.

Obviously strategies will be determined by your own business and industry needs, so think about the things you need to do to achieve your goal.

Tactics

Each strategy will have a series of tactics (or steps) that need to be taken to make that strategy work. As mentioned, these will outline HOW you will go about each strategy. For example.

Key Stratey 2: Decrease expenditure by 15%

2.1 – Review all current suppliers to ensure we are getting the best product for the best price

- 2.1.1 Offer tender opportunitities to new suppliers
- 2.1.2 Research new suppliers via web, phone calls etc
- 2.1.3 Review all suppliers on an annual basis.

2.2 – Introduce new procedures regarding unnecessary printing of emails and other documents to decrease amount of paper being used

2.3 – Re-use single sided documents as scrap paper / memo pads to save paper

2.4 – All electrical equipment and lights to be turned off when not in use

2.5 – Review discounting policy and determine if this could be replaced in a more cost effective manner

2.6 – Review consumable usages

and so on.

Once again, the tactics will depend entirely on what strategies you need to fulfil and should be as detailed as possible. These tactics will form part of your action plan. If there is a cost involved, or extra resources, then detail them here.

Sales Forecast for Next Year

Forecasting is neither as scary nor as complicated as it sounds - if you keep accurate sales records!

Sales forecasting means making an "educated" guess on how much revenue you will earn in the coming year and for this reason accurate records are essential and indispensable. You need to know where your sales came from – by product or service and even by month or week of sale. This may seem overkill but eventually this data will give you a complete and detailed picture of exactly how your business is performing. For example spikes (up or down) in sales figures don't happen for no reason - detailed statistics can show up these spikes which might be due to such things as:

- Promotional or advertising campaigns
- New trends
- New products
- Competitor initiatives
- Seasonal fluctuations
- Economic climates and so on....

For example – the Tourism Industry is very much affected by high and low seasons. They usually know well in advance when demand will increase or decrease. Travelling to Europe in their winter is low season and demand is not as high as going in their spring or summer time. Knowing this tourism operators can plan for these periods by developing specific products designed to increase sales and take advantage of increased demand in high season. They can also accurately forecast revenue because they have a solid knowledge of who their customers are and when they travel on a month by month basis.

The same may well apply to your own industry.

A review of past years sales statistics can give you an excellent idea of how your sales happen on a month by month basis. You can read the trends like a story - allowing you to estimate with a large degree of accuracy what sales you can expect to make and know how much you will need to spend in the next year.

But what good does all this do you in forecasting? When you have collected this data for a number of years you can start to build up a picture of:
- peaks and troughs in your sales
- popular and less popular products,
- popular times of the year
- effects of advertising and/or promotional campaigns and so on

Sales figures rarely drop (or increase) for no good reason.. the trick is to be aware of what is going on around you so that you know why increases or decreases happen. This is where your PLESCT and SWOT prove valuable.

Armed with all this accurate and well researched information you should be able to make a reasonably accurate prediction on how many of each product you will sell in the coming year.

Action Plan

Points for your action plan will come from the tactics. By putting them into an actual action plan, detailing what needs to be done, by whom and by when, you can ensure that each task (or tactic) is done on time and will therefore take you that step closer to reaching your objective.

That, ladies and gentlemen, is basically it!

By following these logical steps you can:
- gain a greater awareness of the environment in which you operate
- avoid major pitfalls that may come your way
- realise your strengths
- overcome weak points
- take advantage of opportunities that are presented to you and much more

Altering Your Business Plan

SWOT diagram:

- **STRENGTH**: What are our resources? What are our resources? What are our resources?
- **WEAKNESS**: Where do we lack? What are our vulnerabilities? What processes can be improved?
- **THREATS**: What are obstacles to our growth? What causes change in demand? Who are the new competitors?
- **OPPORTUNITIES**: What does the market need/want? What are new technologies out there? Who else can we reach?

When – your small farm business plan is done and dusted! But you need to know that Business Plans expire like many foods. They may not spoil but they lose their potency due to changes in business conditions. We will look at five of them.

First, changes in technology impact most businesses. If a new method of doing something is created, the business environment can change very quickly. If your product or service depends on the old technology, your business prospects could be dramatically reduced. Be alert to new technologies that can either hinder or help you. Good examples are the changes from records to tapes, from tapes to cds and from cds to downloadable music on personal players.

Next, consider your customers. If desires change because of some condition, customers could abandon you very quickly. While some customer attrition is normal, be watchful of trends. You don't want to be the last company making buggies and whips when the rest are making automobiles. This doesn't mean you need to be the first to adopt new technology, but stay informed and search out impacts both for the good and bad.

We now come to financial concerns. Similar to losing valued customers, slumping sales figures should be investigated too. It's possible that a temporary condition has caused it, but waiting too long to figure out why and searching for a remedy must be aggressively pursued. The reasons might be found in market conditions, competitors, or the environment. New ways to address the slump must be employed. Your business plans will need to be revised to cope with the changes.

Just like decreasing revenue, increasing costs are destructive. If established cost baselines or forecasts are different, research must be conducted to identify the reasons for the cost changes. Then, remedial steps must be taken to reduce them or make changes to reduce their impact. The investigation should include looking at ways to reduce costs in other areas to help decrease the impact of rising costs. If you are a manufacturing facility, operation efficiency and controlling manufacturing waste can have a large impact on costs too.

Along with decreasing sales, increasing costs, or losing customers growing too quickly can be just as destructive. Explosive growth has many perils to a healthy business. There are challenges in maintaining quality, employing and training employees, procuring raw materials, expanding manufacturing operations and controlling operational costs. Also, it often appears that there are piles of cash coming in so waste and luxuries might accrue. It's a long, known fact that business fail because they succeeded beyond their wildest dreams and aren't able to accommodate the changing conditions successfully.

These five areas require a steady and consistent hand from management. Business plans must constantly be revised to address changing conditions. In a very stable environment, a plan may be stable for a long period, but in an explosive growth environment, the plan might require almost constant review. In any case, the financial and management controls should be monitored constantly to see if changes are occurring and whether they need to be addressed. Recognizing the need to change the governing Business Plan and altering procedures are the modern requirement of a healthy business. An astute management team can address the changing conditions to find new opportunities among the challenges. It is certainly easier to adapt to changing conditions than to have them catch us napping. The latter forcing emergency measures amid a small number of choices, which adds risk to the venture.

PART II: BASICS OF MINI FARMING

In this new world of eco-consciousness, concern of global warming, home business and entrepreneurship, a gourmet treasury of backyard mini-farm opportunities are being born. They range from substantial extra streams of income to full-time income, and from rooftops, even apartments (!) to farms on small acreage. Out of the ashes of the farming disaster in the 1980s came a new form of organic small acreage or backyard farm, the "micro eco-farm." The Centre for the Micro Eco-Farming Movement, there are reports of angora rabbits being raised in apartments, organic herb gardens in backyards selling herbal crafts over the internet, miniature sheep, miniature dairy cows, organic flower farms on small acreage, heirloom vegetable farms on small acreage, garlic farms on small acreage, flower seed farms from backyards, and the list goes on.

Often, they are matched with a home cottage industry, such as spinning wool products from the angora rabbits' wool or teaching cooking classes on the heirloom vegetable farm.

While most of these home businesses are farms from backyards to small acreages, some of these very small farms are within bigger farms. One operates a full time business from two acres, but lives on a 130 acre farm. Another's husband farms huge acreage owned by a corporate farm, but their own seven acres hosts her full time business of growing beautiful herb and flower gardens, growing unusual bedding plants and making gifts from her garden crops for sale in her on-farm gift shop, and hosting weddings and other special events on the farm.

Here's how it works.

In the 80s, as just one example, hundreds of smaller dairy farmers had to go out of business. Cows were injected with hormones to produce massive amounts of milk, and wholesale prices got so cheap, smaller dairy farms just couldn't earn enough from sales anymore. It was get big or get out. Each cow cost more to keep than what was returned. Plus, many of those who used to see milk as nature's most wholesome food began to question its health, and sales dropped even further.

So, how would a micro eco-dairy farm today make money with five cows on a little more than five acres? They raise the cows organically or certified naturally grown on green pasture (the health benefits of this to humans are well-documented, and astounding). With that milk, they handcraft artisan cheese, and sell this premium product often retail to upscale markets for eager buyers seeking healthy, humanely raised grass-fed artisan cheese... cheese in which customers can even name the cows it came from! The cost to keep each cow is returned many times over. Times have changed. Today, hand-tending, handcrafting and allowing customers to reconnect with animals and nature don't work for large-scale agribusinesses, but they work for smaller parcels and have an eager market waiting.

Managing Soil Health: Concepts and Practices

Before getting started on planting a few flowers, you will need to take some time and prepare your garden soil. Clay, silt, and sand will all need to be mixed perfectly in order to prepare your soil to provide the best possible environment for your plants. The ideal soil conditions that will promote excellent plant growth will be 20% clay, 40% silt, and 40% sand. There are many different tests that are used by gardeners that will provide the information you need to know about perfect soil composition. The first of many tests that can be used is to simply put the dirt in your hand and compress it. The soil will need to hold its shape because if it doesn't, the sand ratio is probably off. While you still have the compressed dirt in your hand try to poke it, and if it doesn't fall apart chances are the soil has too much clay.

If you're still confused about the type of soil you have, there is another technique that you can use that will separate each ingredient. Dump a couple of cups of dirt into a bucket of water. If you take the bucket and shake it around for a while, you'll see that the dirt will separate. Let it settle for a little while and you will actually see it separate into three different layers. From the bottom to the top you will see, sand, silt, and clay. At this point you'll be able to determine which of the three you have too much of.

After you've checked, and double-check, and you have found that your soil is low on a certain ingredient, it's time to do something about it. Sand or silt is probably the easiest to deal with because if there is too much, you can always add a little bit of Peat Moss. Also, Peat Moss and sand are an excellent combination if you have too much clay. Peat Moss works really well because when it gets moist it allows the other ingredients to combine a lot easier. If you've played around with the soil to the point where you can't get the right mix, head over to your home improvement center or your hardware store and find a product that can help you determine the quality of your soil. There should be several different products available that can help you.

When working with your garden soil, you'll also want to make note of the water content because this is also important. Water poses the biggest problem if your garden is located in the lowest area of your yard, where all the water drains too. If you have a garden in this area, the best thing to do is raise the garden at least 5 to 7 inches above grade. This will prevent saturation and provide a maximum amount of drainage.

Mixing nutrients with your soil is extremely important at this point, and the reason is many different soils found in urban areas do not contain many of the good nutrients your plans will require. So, at least one to two weeks before planning your garden, you should begin to mix in some fertilizer in your soil. Make sure to mix it in extremely well, and then allowed to sit for a few days. After this is done the soil will be prepped and ready for whatever type of seeds you plan to grow.

The job is not done because even after your seeds have been planted, you will still want to pay attention to what's going on with your soil. You will notice that in the first couple of weeks your seedlings will be using up a lot of the different nutrients around them. This will slowly but surely allow them to sprout into unique plants. You don't want them to run out of food so about a week or two after the initial planting, you'll want to make sure you add at least the same amount of fertilizer as you did before planting your seeds. You want to use your fertilizer sporadically, but you don't want to use it all the time. Rule of thumb for adding fertilizer will typically be every couple of weeks, because this will be plenty to keep your garden green and growing.

When preparing your garden soil the process can be done quite simply by making sure that the soil is more than adequate, if you have a problem with the drainage take care of it, and make sure you have plenty of fertilizer but you don't want to add it all the time. If you follow the directions in this article you will have a wealth of plants that will provide greenery, beauty, or food to eat, in no time at all. If you're having a problem with any of these steps you can always talk to your local nursery, and let them know exactly what you've done so they can help. You'll find that many of the people that work at the plant nursery are very knowledgeable, and willing to help you prepare your garden soil so you can begin to grow some plants.

Steps to Preparing Your New Soil for Planting

Before you start planting your new lawn, you need to take the necessary steps to make your new soil as healthy as possible so that future plants and grasses will be able to grow healthily.

Here are eight steps to get your soil ready for planting.

1. Decide how big your lawn will be

This is the first step and is very important, as many aspects of lawn care require this information. Get a measuring tape and calculate the size of your new lawn.

2. Do a soil test

Send a soil sample to a soil test lab for testing. The result is much more accurate. Basically, you need to know the soil composition and its pH level, which range from 1 to 14. The pH level measure how acidic or alkaline your soil is and for most soil, a pH level of 6.5 to 7.0 is considered ideal and balanced.

3. Adjusting your soil pH

Most of the time, your new soil pH is likely to be off balance. If the test result showed that it is more acidic, you can add limestone to reduce the acidity. On the other hand, if it is too alkaline, you can add sulphur to bring the soil back into balance.

4. Improve your soil texture

If your soil is too sandy, it will not be able to retain water very well. On the other hand, clay soil will be able to retain water very well but due to poor aeration, the water takes a very long time to reach the root level. The ideal soil type is loamy which provide good aeration and water retention capacity. You can add organic matters such as compost to change the texture of your soil. Organic matters can help to loosen and aerate clay soil. They can also help to improve the water holding capacity of sandy soil.

5. Add starter fertilizer

A starter fertilizer is one that you have to work into the soil before planting. It is usually higher in phosphorous than nitrogen and will help the root system to be established in the soil. Adding more phosphorous at this stage is appropriate as phosphorous does not move into the soil with water easily. However, if your soil test indicate that there is already enough phosphorous in the soil, you can switch to another fertilizer with a higher nitrogen concentration.

6. Dig them into the soil

Once you spread the organic matters, the lime or sulfur and starter fertilizer, you will have to use a rototiller to dig all these stuffs into the top four to six inches of the soil. Dig in a crisscross pattern, which ensure that all the materials will be well incorporated into the soil. This digging pattern also breaks up soil clods and big clumps so that your soil is smooth and well aerated.

7. Level the soil

You can use a rake to make your soil smooth and even. You want to get the soil to the right level for sowing seeds or laying sod. If you intend to sow seeds, the soil should be on the same level as your surrounding walk paths or edging. If you are taking the sod route, ensure that the soil level is about 1 inch lower to accommodate the sod thickness.

Pull the rake in a back and forth fashion over a designated area until the soil looks smooth. Then flip the rake over and try to make the soil smoother. As you rake, move backward so that you do not leave your footprint on the new soil.

8. Let the weeds grow first

There may be weed seeds in your new soil now. Water the new soil and let the weeds grow first. Once the weeds appear, uproot them so that they will dry out and die. You may have to do these a couple of time but this process will greatly reduce the number of weeds growing in your lawn in the future.

All new lawns begin with healthy soil. Apply and refine these eight steps to get your new soil ready for planting and you will have a green and lush lawn in the very near future.

9. Enough water but not too much

Another absolutely essential consideration to the health of your plants is water. Plants need enough water - but not too much - to thrive. Too much or too little water will kill your plants.

Gardens located at the bottom of a hill, for example, tend to collect too much water, and may drown your plants. (You do not what drowning victims in your yard!) If your garden is lower than the rest of your yard, consider a raised bed to make sure the soil in it has adequate drainage.

Maintaining your garden properly requires you pay attention to the composition and health of your soil. Be making sure your garden soil remains rich in nutrients and properly hydrated to help the plants flourish.

Creating a Raised Bed

What is raised bed gardening and why should you be interested? It's planting that isn't done directly in the ground. It is -- usually -- done in some kind of raised bed gardening in containers. There are square raised beds, rectangular raised beds, and round raised beds. You can make a raised bed just about any shape you want and, yes, container planters are a form of raised bed.
You don't have to have land the size of Green Acres to garden successfully. You know what I mean -- land stretching out for days.
You also do not have to grow vegetables in the ground. There's nothing out there anywhere that says a veggie garden will only be successful if you have an acre of ground to plant in.

Raised Bed Gardening and the New Homeowner
Let me tell you about my first house and the very first square foot garden I'd ever tended on my own. It was 1991 and I'd just closed on a townhouse in Marlton, New Jersey. It had fenced backyard but the previous owner's dog had really it ripped up.

Now, lots of women may have focused on things like window treatments or furniture.

Not me, boy. The day after closing I went to the home centre and had them cut eight 1x12 pieces of lumber.

For those of you not familiar with the size and dimensions of lumber, the one is the thickness and the 12 is the width. I asked the lumber yard to cut these pieces 4 feet long for two 4x4 square raised beds.

After that, I went over to the garden centre and picked up eight bags of garden soil. Why eight? Because I had no clue as to how much I'd need.

Then I bought some plants and some seed packets. I spent between $30 and $35 for everything.

I learned about raised bed gardening from watching garden shows on TV including Mel Bartholomew's TV show on PBS, "Square Foot Gardening".

Now, I'm not a tool belt diva. I had the rudimentary tools -- hammer, two screwdrivers, and a ratchet set. Hey, how hard can it be to nail four boards together to form a four foot by four foot raised bed garden box?

Harder than I thought.

I either needed someone to hold the lumber while I nailed or needed clamps or a vise. I discovered this after boards came loose and I had littered the air with blue words.

In the end, I got enough nails into the lumber to hold it together (I'm sure my neighbors had a good laugh watching me do this). The pressure of the garden soil also helped keep the shape of the raised bed garden box together.

The point is that raised beds don't have to be works of art -- they don't have to be structurally sound or be able to withstand a 7.3 earthquake. They just have to hold soil.

I grew lots of things in those two raised beds: tomatoes, peppers, cilantro, oregano, squash, beans, dill, basil, eggplant, spinach, musk melon (small cantaloupe), scallions, and fennel.

It's astonishing how much could grow in a small raised bed garden. I also did it with the help of vertical gardening using trellises.

One of the greatest advantages to raised bed gardening is that you control the soil content.

Let's say you've got clay soil like I do here in Tidewater Virginia. Not a problem. Build some raised beds and filled them with a mix of garden soil, compost and something to lighten it up -- vermiculite, perlite, peat moss, or even some sand. One thing you should know is to never use topsoil -- it's too dense and muddy.

I personally use Miracle-Gro products -- I like their water retention mix. Most of their soils have plant food already mixed in and you can buy garden soil, topsoil, and/or potting mix.

Every once in a while, I'll combine garden soil with potting mix because the potting mix already has some perlite in it and this tends to be a lighter, fluffier soil.

One of the things you want to avoid in raised bed or container gardening is heavy soil density. It's like trying to grow plants in wet concrete. The lighter and fluffier it is the easier it will be for plants' roots to grow.

And raised bed gardening does not have to be on the ground. If you have a bad back or you have avoided gardening because you don't want to look like one of those pieces of bent over garden art -- you know the ones, women with fat butts in bloomers -- build your garden beds higher.

You can stack your raised beds on top of each other. Just make sure to anchor the boxes together so that the top box doesn't slip off the bottom. Or you could get wider pieces of lumber to make them higher.

You can grow just about anything in a raised bed. From potatoes to tomatoes to a cutting garden full of zinnias, you can do it in a raised bed.

The only exceptions would be really large-scale shrubs like azaleas and hydrangeas or trees. Although, you could probably plant dwarf trees in them. If you want to grow larger scale veggies like squash, zucchini, melon, or watermelon, you'll probably need most of one end of the raised bed for them to sprawl out in.

Garden Versatility with Raised Bed Gardening

Cultivating soil in a traditional row garden takes time. I don't care if your house is located on the most wonderful loam in the world. It'll still to take time to make it better. Using raised beds allows you to garden instantly.

And you don't have to put to raised beds on dirt or grass. You can place them on a deck or patio. If you do that, I'd either put some kind of bottom on the raised bed box or even set them on pallets (you can sometimes get old pallets from grocery stores for next to nothing).

The point here is when putting a raised bed on a hard surface like concrete; give the plant's roots some air. Make these beds a bit deeper by making the sides of the bed higher -- that allows for plenty of plant growth.

Prevention is Better Than Cure: Dealing With Pests and Diseases

Growing your own vegetables can be very rewarding, but it can also be very frustrating when the pests or diseases get your vegetables first. But there is hope, you can beat the bugs and diseases without using heavy chemicals. Over the years a system called Integrated Pest/Disease Management (IPM)has been developed, where using chemicals is the last resort IPM is based on physical/mechanical, biological and chemical controls measures.

Physical/mechanical means that you pull weeds out by hand, you squash aphids between your fingers, or use a spade to dig out weeds. Biological controls means using other insects/animals to control the one/s that are out of control. For example using predaory mites to control two spotted mite on azaleas. And the last is chemical control which is using sprays to eliminate the pests or diseases. Using chemicals should always be the last resort.

Putting the right plant in the right position in well prepared soil is also another tactic in trying to combat pest and diseases. If plants are in the right spot, they will be healthy and strong, but if you put them in the wrong position, they become susceptible to pests and diseases. Providing them with right conditions, allows them to build up their vigour and strength and that helps protect them from attack. Make sure your plants are receiving the right amounts of water they need. Too much or little can cause plants to become stressed and this lower their resistance to attack from pests and pathogens. Pests seem to know they are stressed!

Another method to help reduce the build up pests and diseases is crop rotation. To ensure that this method works properly, you need to understand what families vegetables come from. Vegetables from the same families attract similar pests and diseases.

Family Groupings

The following chart groups the vegetables in their families for you. By knowing this you will be able to plan your vegetables beds accordingly.

Family Name | Botanical Name | Common Name
- Amaranthaceae Beta vulgaris Beetroot
- Amaranthaceae Beta vulgaris var. cicla Silverbeet
- Amranthaceae Beta vulagais Mangel Wurzel
- Apiaceae Daucus carota Carrots
- Apiaceae Pastinaca sativa Parsnips
- Apiaceae Apium graveolens var.dulce Celery
- Apiaceae Apium graveolens var.rapaceum Celeriac

- Asparagaceae Asparagus officinalis (Monocot = grasses) Asparagus
- Asteraceae Cynara scolymus Globe Artichoke
- Asteraceae Helianthus tuberosus(root vegetable)Jerusalem Artichoke
- Asteraceae Lactuca sativa Lettuce

- Brassicaecea Brassica oleracea Cauliflower
- Brassiceacea Brassica oleracea Italica Grp Broccoli
- Brassicaceae Brassica oleracea CapitataGrp Cabbage
- Brassicaceae Brassica oleracea GemmiferaGrp Brussels Sprouts
- Brassicaceae Brassica oleracea Acephala Grp Kale
- Brassicaceae Raphanus sativus Radish
- Brassicaceae Spinacia oleracea Spinach
- Brassicaceae Brassica rapa Turnip
- Cucurbitaceae Cucumis sativus Cucumber
- Cucurbitaceae Cucurbita maxima Pumpkins
- Curcubitaceae Cucumis melo Canteloupe
- Curbutitaceae Cucurbiat pepo Squash, Zucchini and Gourds

- Lilaceae Allium cepa Onions
- Lilaceae Allium sativum Garlic
- Lilaceae Allium ameloprasum Leaks

- Poaceae Zea mays(Monocot = grasses) Sweet Corn
- Polygonaceae Rheum x hybrdum Rhubarb

- Solanaceae Capsicum spp. Capsicum and Chillies
- Solanaceae Lycopersicon esculentum Tomatoes
- Solanaceae Solanum tuberosum Potatoes
- Solanaceae Solanum melongena Eggplants

Pests and Diseases

Vegetables attract their fair share of pests and diseases and if you are growing a lot of one crop (called monoculture), pests and diseases are highly attracted to them. To confuse the pests, it is a good idea to interplant your vegetables. For example planting silver beet around the cauliflower or broccoli. This does make practicing crop rotation difficult, unless you have planned really well what's going where.

There are two types of pests, chewing ones such as snails and caterpillars and sap sucking ones such as aphids. They are controlled by different chemical methods. There are two types of chemicals - contact and systemic. Contact chemicals only work when the pest is there and washes off with rain or watering. It is important to understand that many of the homemade remedies or less stronger chemicals' such as pyrethrin or Dipel are contact sprays. They only last a day or two made up in the bottle, so don't make large amounts and store it as they lose their potency. Systemic on the other hand are absorbed by the leaf and move around the leaves vascular system. They are much stronger chemicals and last in the plant for a lot longer but you may not want to use them on vegetables you are going to eat.

It is also important that if you are making your own remedies, that all the utensils you use are kept separate from the kitchen utensils. Remember home-made remedies can be poisonous to you too!

Home-made and less toxic Chemical Remedies to Control Pests and Diseases

Flying insects and Caterpillars

Sticky traps for whitefly, aphids, thrips and leaf miner moths. Light traps are good for catching tomato grub moths and lawn armyworm. Steel wool can be placed around tree trunks to prevent ants farming insects such as scale, aphids and mealy bugs because they produce a sticky substance called honeydew.

Snail bait does not work on caterpillars. They are controlled by less harmful poisons such as Dipel or Pyrethrum (Long Life). These are contact sprays and need to be reapplied after rain or watering. There are also many homemade recipes for controlling pests and diseases.

Garlic spray can be used to control aphids and caterpillars in the garden. It is a contact spray. Soak 1 bulb of finely chopped garlic, in paraffin for 3 days. Dissolve 2 cups of soap flakes in 1L. of water and add to the garlic mixture. Stand the mixture for a further 2 days and the strain mixture through pantihose. Dilute 1/2cup of garlic concentrate with 4L. of water before application.

Chilli spray can be used for control of chewing insects and aphids. Can also control possums until they get used to the taste. It is a contact spray. Blend 40 fresh chilli peppers in 1L. of water. Add 5g. of pure soap flakes to blended chilli mixture. Apply as required undiluted.

Oil sprays can be used to control scale, aphids, mealy bugs, mites and thrips. Vegetable oil and light mineral oils such as paraffin are permitted for use in 'certified organic farming'. Petroleum based oils known as 'White Oil or All Seasons Oil' is not permitted in 'certified organic farming'. Do not use any oil spray if the maximum daily temperature is going to be over 23C as they can burn the plants leaves. Also causes burning if used within 4 weeks of using a sulphur spray such as wettable sulphur or lime sulphur.

Mix 1tbsp of liquid soap with 1 cup of vegetable oil. Dilute as required using 1-2.5tsp of the mixture to 1 cup of water.

Snails and Slugs

Snails are a big pest. There are several methods to prevent them attaching your seedlings and plants.

DO NOT USE SNAIL BAIT IF YOU HAVE A DOG. SNAIL BAIT IS ATTRACTIVE TO DOGS BECAUSE IT HAS BRAN IN IT AND IS POISONOUS TO THEM.

You can sprinkle crushed eggshells, sharp sand around it each plant. Be careful using hydrated lime and wood ash as both are alkaline and can alter your soil's pH.After it has rained, go out and pick them up and put them in the bin. Also check under pots for slugs and any nice damp place for snails to hide.

Fungicides
Sulphur is used to control powdery mildew and vegetables, fruit trees and ornamentals, rust on vegetables and fungal diseases on stone fruit. It is a protectant, eradicate, contact spray.

Sulphur should not be used 21 days before or after using an oil spray, or in combination with an oil spray or over 23C. It can be purchased as 'Sulfur Spray', 'Dusting sulphur', 'Powdered Sulphur' or 'Wettable Sulphur'.

Copper based products such as 'Kocide' and 'Bordeaux' are used as a protective spray against many bacterial and fungal diseases that affect fruit trees, vegetables and ornamental plants.

In winter,you can spray roses with lime sulphur to control the fungal disease black spot. It kills the black spot spores. You can spray the soil around the plant and stems and leaves of the bush. To prevent burning the new spring foliage, make sure you spray before the new leaves have emerged.

Weeds
Boiling water can be used to kill small weeds growing in between bricks and paving and some ant species. However, this method does not work on bulbous weeds such as oxalis, as energy stored in the bulb, allows it to grow new leaves.

Vinegar, salt and water can also be used to kill weeds. This is a spray best used once or twice because if you continually use it on the same spot, the build-up of salt in the soil could cause salination problems.

It is important to remember that all chemical sprays, whether commercially manufactured or home-made need to be handled carefully and stored responsibly. It is important to read the directions on commercially produced chemicals on how to use them safely and understand the Withholding Period (number of days that must pass before you can harvest the produce) if you are spraying them onto your vegetables. If you make your own home remedies, it is a good idea to label the spray bottle with the name of the product and date it was made. NEVER STORE ANY CHEMICALS IN SOFT DRINK BOTTLES as children can mistake the liquid for a drink. Make sure your chemicals are in a shed or cupboard that locks and keeps children and pets out!

Pests and diseases are a challenge when growing vegetables, but don't give up. All gardens have problems and you will build up knowledge as you get more experience. The effort is worth it as home-grown vegetables are out of this world and taste brilliant.

Seed Starting

You want to decide beforehand which vegetable seeds you wish to plant. Before you select the seeds do some research as some vegetables cannot be sowed until the last frost has passed. Basically, this means that some garden vegetable seeds, such as onions and carrots for example, cannot be started indoors but must be started in the ground.

Gather all of your necessary supplies for the indoor garden. You can use small pots or containers, or to make things a little easier yourself you can purchase seed starter kits. The seed starter kits are an easy way to learn indoor planting. Many of these kits include soil pellets. If you do not have adequate sunlight inside your home for your garden vegetable seeds than also purchase a grow light; these can be found at any home and garden store.

With all of your supplies and vegetable seeds ready to plant, first check your growing zone. It is ideal to wait until a month or two before the last frost date of your growing zone to plant your garden vegetable seeds indoors. The reason for this is that the vegetables will have a good start by the time the spring season arrives.

When you begin to plant your vegetable seeds, consider the size of the garden that you wish to grow. Once you take that into consideration, plant extra seeds to the already estimated amount. Because when you transport the plants into your garden, the stress caused to the plants during the process might make you lose some of the plants.

Now it's time to add the soil. If you have decided to purchase soil pellets, be sure to read the directions. However, the basic instructions are to allow the pellets to expand by soaking them, placing one seed into each pellet and add water every day. If you're using the traditional method, place the soil into the pot or container and then place one or two seeds inside of each pot. It's best to place two seeds just in case if one of the seeds doesn't make it to the growing phase.

Place the garden vegetable seeds under a grow light or a designated sunny location. Be sure that you check the soil every day to see if it needs water. Never let the soil become dry but at the same time never let it get too wet. Healthy soil is firm and moist. Eventually you will notice your garden vegetable seeds starting to sprout. Continue to provide care and maintenance to your garden vegetable seeds inside the house until the risk of frost has passed.

You will need to get the plants accustomed to being outside. You do this by taking them outside a week to two weeks before you plan to plant them in the ground. You continue to make daily checks and to provide water as needed. By waiting 1-2 weeks this gives you a chance to quickly bring them back inside if the weather gets close to the freezing mark or frost begins to appear.

When it's time to plant them in the ground, place both the seedling and the soil into the ground. Be mindful that you don't pull the roots because it will cause them to break. After this point the plants of your garden vegetable seeds are sensitive and can easily dry out and begin to die. So make sure that you water them regularly after transplanting.

Guide to Growing Fruit Trees and Vines

It's a great feeling to walk into the garden and be able to pick a basket of tasty fresh fruit that you have grown yourself. No longer are you at the mercy of commercial growers having to have only the varieties that they decide to offer. You can choose the fruit that you want and know that it will be much tastier.

Peaches, apricots, nectarines and plums grown for the supermarkets are often picked so green then cooled and stored for so long that they do not ripen correctly and we are unable to enjoy their true taste. With the present economic climate tightening our purse strings, along with the guidelines on health issues being reported daily on how and what to eat, there is no better time than now to start growing your own delicious healthy fruit. You don't need a huge backyard to cultivate your favorite fruit, as containers can be used very successfully. However, it should be remembered that plums, pears, apples and cherries need another variety close by for pollination so you need to plan for a couple of trees of each variety. There are many dwarf stocks available to suit a small garden; although they will produce fruit of normal size in 3 to 5 years you won't get the same quantity as from a standard sized tree.

Growing fruit trees in containers is a relatively easy exercise, and pruning and harvesting is also much easier. Containers are manufactured from plastic, clay, wood, metal etc; there is sure to be one that will be suitable for you. There are many varieties of fruit which can be grown successfully in containers in a small garden or placed on a balcony. This is very useful for people with small or even no garden.

If you decide to use pots because of limited space issues, remember you need to have a pot about 6 inches bigger than the pot which holds the tree when you buy from the garden centre. Repot one size up every two years. Well drained sandy, fertile soil is generally suitable for dwarf fruit trees; your garden centre will advise on what is most suitable. As with all plants, suitable light conditions apply, so make sure they get the benefit that maximum sunlight will give. Your dwarf tree can even be moved inside in cold spells.

Regular pruning is necessary for proper care of most fruit trees. To maintain the shape of your miniature fruit tree light pruning to remove broken or diseased branches can be done any time of the year. Thinning out early summer time or alternatively in September after you've harvested the fruit is ideal to get the desired shape for your fruit tree and to restrict undesired growth. However, the main removal of branches is much easier to do in winter when they are dormant, as they are much more accessible without their leaves and you can see what you're doing. Just make sure this is completed before growth starts again in spring. During the growing season, fertilize every 4-6 weeks. When watering your dwarf fruit trees, let the surface dry out a little before adding more water.

Yet another way for the small garden owner to grow his own fruit is to use a form of pruning called "Espaliering" which allows you to train the trees branches laterally, or even to the shape of a fan, and so you can grow your fruit against a wall or garden fence. There are many different shapes that the espalier may take. Apples and pears adapt very well to this style of training, however other fruit trees such as plums, cherries, peaches, nectarines, almonds, apricots and fruiting vines can also be espaliered with great success. The overall effects are stunning, the best reward from this type of pruning being when they are in flower. Also the fruit is a picture to behold, and sometimes it's a shame to have to pick the fruit. An advantage of growing espaliers is that it is much easier to pick the fruit and its also easier using netting to protect your delicious fruit. Espaliered trees have the same growing requirements as other fruit and deciduous trees; they need adequate watering in summer and fertile soil conditions are essential to maintaining a healthy tree.

Initially you need to regularly prune and tie in the branches to create the flat shape. When the desired shape and size are reached, this must be maintained with regular pruning; winter is the best time for this job when the tree is dormant. Make sure the lower branches get their fair of sunshine by pruning the excessive growth in early summer.

Raising Chickens for Eggs

Can raising chickens help your finances? Yes it can. Raising chickens is more than just fresh eggs!

If you want to have fresh eggs, and make some extra money, then raising chickens might be for you.

My parents raised chickens once they became retired and they loved it. They lived in town but the city ordinance allowed chickens to be kept in the back yard.

They also planted a garden so using the old chicken manure was helpful, not to mention free. Saving money is the same as making money!

I can remember the wonderful taste of those fresh eggs still today, but mom and dad did more with their chickens. They bought a small incubator and some of the eggs were hatched and the baby chicks were sold for extra profits. Baby chicks really sell good around the Easter holiday.

Also the eggs were sold to neighbours for extra money. I have also known people that sell their eggs to small mom and pop grocery stores. You could even rent a small vender's cart and sell your fresh eggs to the public. Be sure and get legal advice in permits first.

Chickens usually lay one egg every day, so depending on how many dozen eggs you need a week, you can decide how many chickens to raise. If you just want eggs for yourself, then about three to five chickens will give you more than enough eggs.

If your chicken quits being a good laying hen then you can eat the chicken. Most people don't eat their chickens however because they become like pets. Some like to be held and petted like a dog or cat!

Most importantly, chickens are low maintenance so this is a easy way to put back some extra money for that vacation you have been wanting to take!

Raising chickens for eggs can be far more beneficial than just producing your own eggs. They also make great pets, are very friendly if you raise them correctly, and will give you and your children many hours of fun and amusement.

There are five basic steps to raising chickens for eggs.

1. The first thing you need to do when making the decision to raise chickens for eggs is to find out if you are allowed by law to keep chickens in your back yard. This varies significantly around the world. For example in New York City you can have as many chickens as you like but you are not allowed to have roosters because their crowing may disturb your neighbours. In London you are also allowed to keep chickens but in some cities it is totally banned. There is a growing movement of people protesting in these cities so that they too can enjoy the experience of raising chickens for eggs.

2. Look at the space you have available in your yard. Chickens do not need a lot of room but the size of the chicken run will determine the number of chickens you will be able to raise. It is not necessary to have a huge flock and if you are just starting out I would recommend 3 to 6 chickens. This will allow you to manage your flock easily and as laying chickens will produce approximately one egg each per day, you will have plenty of eggs.

3. The chicken coop is your next consideration. You can buy readymade chicken coops or you can make your own. A simple steel garden shed can be converted into a chicken house and recently I saw a children's cubby house that was no longer being used, converted into a great chicken coop. There are some really inventive coops around, let your imagination run free. You need to make sure your chickens are protected from the weather, have a place to roost at night and have some nesting boxes to lay their eggs in. Also they need to be locked in every night so that predators can't get to them. This is very important.

4. Ordering your chickens is next. Do you want to raise them from baby chicks or do you want chickens that are ready to lay. Baby chicks are more time consuming and you have to wait for them to grow up before you get your eggs, but children find them irresistible and can develop relationships with them right from the start. However if you are new to raising chickens then I would recommend you buy hens that are ready to lay. You can get them at your local fodder store or you can order them and have them delivered to your door depending of course on where you are in the world.

5. Enjoying your chickens is the next step. Make sure they have fresh clean water, this is very important for their health. If you want to save time, you can buy automatic waterer's that will ensure they have fresh water all the time. You just hook the waterer up to a hose and the chickens will always have clean water. They need feeding every day with grain or pellets and all your kitchen and garden scraps. Providing them with scraps and green food i.e. weeds, is the secret to producing great tasting eggs. You can also save time by having automatic feeders as well but I find that I end up feeding the local bird population as well if I do this so I prefer to feed them daily myself when I collect the eggs. Scattering grain and scraps around their yard is not difficult.

There are so many reasons to raise chickens for eggs. Join the growing trend and turn your urban yard into a food producing haven. The next step is to grow your own vegetables, but that is another story on the way to sustainable living and you may not have the room or the inclination. A good start however is to get your own chickens and see how you go from there. If nothing else you will get great tasting eggs and a great deal of satisfaction from raising chickens for eggs.

Raising Chickens for Meat

Before you go out and buy some chickens for meat, you need to do some research. There many things to consider before you take the plunge. This guide will help you so you don't have any unexpected surprises. These steps helped us raise 44 meat chickens that averaged out to 7.25 pounds in just nine weeks.

Step 1: Should you Raise Meat Chickens?
This is a step every new farmer needs to decide. They are very different to raise than egg laying chickens. Usually you will have quite a few at a time, which means a lot more chicken manure, and feed costs. Also you need to decide on which type of meat chicken you want to raise. Also, if you get easily attached, you have to be able to face the fact that these birds are only going to live about 8-10 weeks before processing. These chickens can't live comfortably much longer as they grow so fast.

The most popular type of meat chicken is commonly known as a Cornish cross. These chickens are a cross between a Cornish and a White Rock. They are used in factory farms, and small family run operations across the country. They are known for their efficient feed to weight ratio, making them one of the cheapest chickens to raise. They are usually ready to process between 8-10 weeks old, weighing anywhere from 5-8 pounds.

Another option is freedom rangers. They take a bit longer, about 12 weeks, but are much more adaptable to foraging, and free ranging. They are a very hardy bird, and grow to about 6-7 pounds in 12 weeks.

Where Do I Buy Meat Chickens?
If you lucky enough to have a hatchery close by, then you can simply go buy them there. But, if your like most people, the internet is going to be your answer. We ordered ours from Murray McMurray Hatchery. We couldn't have been happier with the service, and all chickens arrived alive and well. There are many different hatcheries around the country. Read the reviews that people leave, and should give you an idea what kind of service to expect.

Step 2: Raising Baby Chicks
Now that you have chicks coming through the mail in a small box, you need to think about their home for the next few weeks. You will need to set up a brooder, feed and water, and keep them clean in order to keep them healthy.

Setting up Your Brooder
A brooder is a place to keep your birds contained, clean and warm. It is usually a container, with shavings on the bottom, a brooding light up above, and their food and water containers. You can make the brooder yourself, don't need anything fancy here. Usually a container, more than 12" high, and you won't need a top.

Brooding Lamp

The brooding light is a 250 watt red light, in a reflective housing that will provide heat for the chicks, since they don't have feathers to keep them warm. It's also good to find the lights with a wire guard on the bottom will help protect from fires in case it falls onto the shavings.

You'll also need to figure out the height of the lamp to adjust for temperature. This can easily be done by attaching the light to a chain with an S hook. Each week you'll plan on adjusting the temperature down 5 degrees so help the birds adjust.

Start with a temperature of about 95-100 for day old chicks, and back it off slowly over the weeks. Also watch how your birds react. If they huddle around the light, then lower it some. If they run away then pull it up some so it isn't so hot for them. Also find a comfy area for their food and water so they don't overheat or get chilled when they eat.

Thermometer

You will want a thermometer to keep an eye on the temperature. I find the best ones to use are those used to watching food temperatures. The type with a probe on a wire attached to a separate base. That way you only have to have a metal probe down in, and the chicks can't hurt it.

Bedding

For the first few days paper towels work great, because the chicks tend to want to eat the shavings. Then switch to pine shavings, a few inches thick. Avoid cedar as it is toxic to poultry. Make sure there is enough shavings to keep them dry, and to avoid the slippery bottom, because they could slip and hurt their legs.

Feeders and Waterers

There are many kinds of feeders out there, or you could use bowls and plates. Choose one that works for you. We use tower types. The base unscrews and allows you to fill with water and feed. These will usually last you through the day pretty easily.

Step 3: Choosing A Coop
While your chicks are growing, you need to decide on a coop. There are a couple different types, and features to consider. Depending on what you have for space, and how you want to raise your chickens should help you decide.

Chicken Coop with Run
This is a more permanent design. You will have to build a chicken coop, and give them a fenced in area outside to run around in. You will need 2-3 square feet inside the coop, and about 4 square foot outside in the run. If they are cooped all the time, give about 5 square foot.

Wagon Type Chicken Tractor
If you are able to completely free range your chickens, this method will be best for you. It involves building a chicken coop on a trailer, or wagon frame. You then can move it with either a small tractor, or even an ATV. The same 2-3 square foot rule applies. Your chickens will go in on their own at night, and you'll close it up to protect them from predators. Then in the morning you move them to a new spot, open the door and let them range and forage.

Movable Tractor With Run

Most people use this method, including me, to raise their meat chickens. It involves an open style wire pen, with one end closed in to provide some shelter. We gave ours 2 square foot of room throughout. This type can be moved by hand, usually with a hand truck to lift one end, and drag along the other end. Usually you only have to move once per day, but as the birds get larger we moved twice per day so provide more grass, and keep them out of their manure. See out step by step design chicken tractor.

Step 4: Introducing Your Chickens To Chicken Tractor

Now that your chicks have feathered out they are old enough to go outside. Usually late spring is the best time to put birds outside because the temperature isn't too hot or cold, but that depends on your location too.

Feeding

Now that your birds are outside, and getting larger you need bigger feeders and waterers. These are usually in the 5 gallon pail size, but there are many variations. You need to select a size that works with your schedule so they always have fresh water, and feed won't run out.

A good rule of thumb is 12 hours with feed, 12 without. We find the birds will forage more in the morning when we first move the tractor, allowing them to take in those nutrients, and fill up some on grass helping to cut feed costs. Your local feed store can help you decide on the right grain mix, usually called broiler grower.

Health and Sickness

Don't be surprised if you do lose a bird or two, maybe more throughout their lives. It's just a fact of life for these chickens. But you can keep a close eye on them, and try to isolate the birds from the others. Keep a close eye especially when they first go to a chicken tractor, as this is the most stressful time in their lives. If a chicken seems tired, or looks droopy, bring them back in and keep your eye on them. Vet costs are usually too much to make it worthwhile for these short life chickens.

Step 5: Processing
Now all your hard work is finally ready to pay off. Your chickens now are about 8-10 weeks old, and much longer their hearts and legs will start to give out, and they begin to suffer. This is where you decide to bring them somewhere else to get processed, or do it yourself.

Butchering Your Own Chickens
Unless you are going to do a lot of birds, the start-up cost can be substantial. It is also not for the faint of heart. You first need to kill them quickly, dunk them in hot water, get their feathers off, gut them and package them. But if this is something you are going to do for a very long time, or like knowing that everything was done on our farm, this would be the way to go. You can cut out the additional cost, and stress on the birds of bringing them to a butcher.

Hiring out for Processing
An easier way to finish your birds is to bring them to a butcher shop. The best way to find local processors is to talk to your neighbourhood farmers and get their opinions. You want to make sure they are clean, and professional. You will be eating this food, so do your research. Also talk to them about costs, and packaging. Most will come vacuum sealed, and for chickens the cost is per bird.

The Final Word

All this may seem kind of intense, but if you follow this guide, you will have a good understanding to raise your own chickens. You too can raise good size chickens that will have more flavour, put money in your pocket, and give you the pride of knowing you did it yourself. So instead of buying that chicken on the shelf, why don't you think about raising it at home.

Too Much Harvest, Not Enough Time

It is quite common for new gardeners to go all out planning and planting their first garden or two, having no idea what will grow, how much it will grow, and what you will do with the harvest you get. Planning is an important part to having a successful garden harvest and knowing what to do with it at the end of the summer.

Planning what to do with your garden harvest really starts in the spring, when you are planning what to plant, but you may need to grow a garden or two in your area to get a sense for what grows well, and what you can put up for the winter months. If you do not want to deal with trial and error you can always ask your neighbours that garden what grows best in your area. Once you know what grows best in your climate it will be time to take some steps to be sure you maximize your harvest at the end of the year.

Sell Immediately
Look for local farmer's markets and get set up with your own booth. Often the cost to sell is quite low or even free. Just be sure you find out about any requirements and regulations beforehand.

With these ideas your vegetable gardening efforts can reward you in veggies, friends, and even money.

Share
Many backyard gardeners innately know to share their harvest with family, friends, and neighbors. This is a great way to spread the excitement of vegetable gardening with people we see every day. Co-workers are also naturally included in our sharing circle. This is a great way to connect with people and share our gardening experience firsthand.

Do not Plant Anything Your Family Will Not Eat
This is an important point, we sometimes get carried away with wanting to grow lots of food, not taking into account whether our family will eat it or not. If your family hates spinach do not grow it.

Read up on Preserving Methods

If you do not know how you will be putting up your food for the winter now is the time to find out before you plant. This too will affect what you plant and how much you will plant of each food. If you plan to can your vegetables for instance you may want to plant more corn, beans and carrots, and less squash and lettuce that cannot be canned. Canning and freeze complement each other well, as some things are better canned while others are better frozen.

Make a list of What You are Canning or Freezing
Understand the differences between the two and have a well-orchestrated plan based on what you will do with each part of your harvest. For instance you may know you may want to use or sell some of your cucumbers fresh, but what will you do with the rest? How about relish or bread and butter pickles? Beans are best fresh or canned so plan to do both, and corn can be preserved either way and is wonderful fresh so if you have the room you can never go wrong planting lots of corn.

Gather Supplies Early
Once you have a clear idea of what you are going to do with your harvest it is time to gather your supplies, stores run out of canning supplies early on so it is best not to wait till the heat of the canning season to buy them. If you know what you will need buy them before they are gone.

Preserve as you Pick
Do not get behind, let your vegetables sit after harvest, or stay on the plants too long. You will risk losing your harvest or allow your vegetables to be past their prime when you can or freeze them. This can be very disappointing and discouraging for a buyer when their home grown foods do not come as nice as they hoped they would.

Be sure you have Adequate Storage Space

Nothing is a disheartening as freezing all your harvest only to get to the end of your season and have no place to put the rest of your harvest. By planning carefully you can balance what you can with what you freeze to insure you will have enough room for everything.

PART III: GETTING THE MOST OUT OF YOUR VEGGIES

If you are going to be successful in mini farm business then one skill that you will have to master is how to put your time to best use. In fact being able to prioritise your daily activities and dedicate adequate time to it can be very difficult to achieve sometimes, as diversions and other distractions knock you off course. However, there are a few basic things that you can do that will help you stay on track and get the most out of you working day.

Soil and Fertility

Soil is an end-product of rock weathering into finely divided material mixed with organic matter that can support vegetation. There are three forms of rock weathering: physical weathering, chemical weathering and biological weathering. Soil is then formed in stages. The first stage is the accumulation of weathered rock fragments. The second stage is the formation of layers, called horizons. The layers run parallel to the grounds surface and are made up of like material, having similar structure, particle size, texture and porosity. The horizons differ from the layers above and below each other. The third stage is called humification. That is the process of growth and death of lichens, fungi and plants along with bacterial action to add organic content to the soil. The upper horizon is called topsoil and as gardeners this is the area we will be dealing with the most. Soils that have the three fully developed horizons are known as mature soils. Different soil characteristics are developed by rainfall, profusion of plants, drainage, temperature, topography and the mineral contents of the rocks that originally formed the soil.

Soil Structure

The inorganic or mineral elements of soils are particles of varying size. From the largest to the smallest, soil components are divided into three types: sand, silt and clay. The four main classes of soil texture are loam, clay, peat and alluvium.

- Loam is a texture with sand, silt and clay in an even balance, with a high percentage of organic material.
- Clay is a texture with at least 20% or greater clay particles.
- Peat is a deposit of partially decomposed organic matter that has been preserved by the lack of oxygen through water saturation.
- Alluvium is fine grained soil of silt and mud particles deposited by streams or rivers.

Experienced soil testers can tell what type and texture of soil you have by hand. They see if the soil will ball up in their hand and they rub the soil in the palm of their hands to further identify type and texture. Of course this is just their observations that back up the lab analysis. Soil structure affects the ability of soil to hold air and moisture uniformly and the ability of root structures to develop.

Soil Nutrients

Soil nutrients are essential for plant growth and development. The mineral nutrients are present in solution in the soil water, where it is taken in and up by the plants root system. The plant nutrients are divided into two main categories: macronutrients and micronutrients. The macronutrients are needed in large quantities and are as follows: carbon, oxygen, hydrogen, nitrogen (chemical symbol N), phosphorus (P), potassium (K), calcium (Ca), magnesium (Mg), and sulfur (S). Carbon, oxygen and hydrogen are found in the air and water, with all the others found in mineral form. Calcium (Ca), magnesium (Mg), and sulfur (S) are also known as Secondary Nutrients. Plants need these three secondary nutrients in the same amounts as the others but most soils are not deficient in these macronutrients. The three we will be dealing with the most are nitrogen (N), phosphorus (P) and potassium (K), with nitrogen being in inadequate amounts in most garden soils. The micronutrients are; iron (Fe), zinc (Zn), manganese (Mn), boron, copper, molybdenum, and chlorine. The micronutrients are also known as the trace elements since they are only needed in small quantities. Excess amounts of trace elements can be toxic to plants.

Soil pH

Soil acidity or alkalinity is indicated by the soil pH value. Soil ranges from acid to neutral to alkaline. The pH scale ranges from zero to 14 with 7 being neutral, zero being the highest acid reading with 14 being the most alkaline. If the pH analysis is high in either direction, key nutrients can be chemically "tied up" or insoluble to the soils water, thus not available for take up by the plants root system. Most plants like a slightly acidic soil. The pH range preferred by most garden plants is about 6.0 pH to 7.2 pH. Acid soil is common in heavy rainfall areas and is frequently associated with sandy soils and soils high in organic material. Adding lime (calcium carbonate) is usually recommended to raise pH if your soil is acidic. Alkaline soil is usually found in areas of low rainfall and high calcium carbonate. Sulphur can be added to lower pH or you can amend your soil over time with compost or aged manure. Be careful if you are using fresh or green manure as this can lead to excessive salt in the soil which will pull water from the plants roots.

Soil Testing

A soil analysis will determine your nutrient levels and your soils pH. Many DIY soil testing kits are available through Ace hardware, Lowe's or your local gardening centre. Rapitest is a brand that is widely used and is readily available online at Park Seeds. The costs vary and you want to make sure what your kit does or does not test for. Most kits do not include the pH test but it can be purchased separately. The most accurate and complete analysis comes from a analytical laboratory. You can contact your extension service through this link and it will have your state extension office information. Some extension offices have a lab for testing and all of them will have lists of qualified laboratories in your home area. You can also order a soil analysis test with micronutrient audit online from Peaceful Valley Farm and Garden Supply. It is a very accurate and complete test and like the others, information will be given on how to collect the sample for testing. You can see the importance of having accurate information on your gardens soil. When you know what you have and what your soil may be in need of you can then make positive amendments to your soil that will help your plants flourish.

Asparagus

Asparagus (Asparagus officinalis) is a member of the lily family. It has been grown for more than 2,000 years and is quite popular in the home garden today. On the other hand Asparagus is an excellent source of vitamin A and contains significant levels of calcium, phosphorus, riboflavin, thiamine and Vitamin C.

Asparagus characteristics
Asparagus is a perennial and will produce for many years when properly planted and maintained. It has underground storage roots and compact stems called rhizomes. The roots store food and the rhizomes produce edible shoots or asparagus spears. If the spears are not harvested, they rapidly develop into fern-like bushes 4 or more feet tall. The foliage produces carbohydrates, which is again stored in the roots.

Asparagus has both male and female plants. Both sexes flower and the female plants produce small, round, red berries in the fall. Female plants do not live as long or produce as well as male plants.

Asparagus climatic requirements

Asparagus is a cool-season vegetable and prefers cool temperatures without frosts throughout the growing season. It is better adapted to the Cumberland Plateau and the high elevations of East Tennessee than to West Tennessee, but will survive and produce significant yields throughout the state given a suitable location.

Asparagus best location

It is best to locate asparagus plantings to the side of the vegetable garden with other perennials such as rhubarb, strawberries and brambles. This will keep the plants away from cultivation and other gardening activities. Asparagus should be planted where it will receive a minimum of seven or eight hours of sunlight on sunny days. North or east slopes are preferable to south or west slopes, as they are slower to warm in the spring. Early developing asparagus spears are frequently killed by late freezes.

Asparagus soil

Asparagus will survive in any well-drained soil. The best soils for asparagus are deep and loose, such as sandy loams. Heavy-textured clays and shallow soils should be avoided, since they restrict root development and promote root rots. Extremely sandy soils may not retain enough moisture for vigorous asparagus growth. Soils that warm up quickly in the spring promote early growth and harvest. This may be a disadvantage, as developing asparagus spears grow slowly in very cold weather and will be killed to the ground by freezes. Asparagus grows best on soils with a pH of 6.0 to 6.5.

Asparagus varieties

'Martha Washington' is an old, standard asparagus variety. 'Mary Washington' appears to be a newer, improved cultivar. 'Purple Passion' is a relatively new variety with very large spears and a high sugar content.

In the last few years there have been many new hybrid asparagus varieties released. These varieties usually produce all or nearly all male plants. This increases their yield, because male plants produce about 25 percent more than female plants and because of hybrid vigour.

Asparagus fertilizer and lime

Asparagus grows best on soils with a pH of 6.0-6.5. Take a soil sample to determine lime, phosphate and potash levels before planting. In addition, before spears emerge in the spring and after harvest, annually supplement the above fertilizer recommendations with one pound of ammonium nitrate or its equivalent per 100 square feet of asparagus bed.

Asparagus planting and spacing

Plant asparagus early in the spring while it is still dormant, usually in February or early March.

Asparagus plants can be started from seed, but this is not recommended for home gardeners. Germination of asparagus seed is slow and weeds can be difficult to control. Plants grown from seed are transplanted to a permanent bed the following spring; so asparagus grown from seed also requires a longer time to begin bearing.

It is preferable to purchase 1-year old dormant crowns. This will cut the time before harvest by at least one year and eliminate caring for the tiny seedlings the first year.

Dig a trench 6 to 8 inches deep and place the crowns in the bottom. Space the plants 15 to 18 inches apart and leave 3 to 4 feet between rows. Spread the roots evenly and cover them with 2 to 4 inches of soil. Fill the remainder of the trench after the plants begin growth.

Do not try and fill in skips in an old planting with young plants, as the remaining old plants will inhibit the growth of smaller, younger plants. If seedlings appear in an old planting, they are best pulled out or transplanted to another area.

Asparagus irrigation

During the first growing season, apply sufficient water to wet the soil 1 foot deep once a week. If it doesn't rain, this may require as much as 1 inch of water. After the first growing season, watering every other week is usually sufficient. A 2-inch layer of an organic mulch such as shredded leaves or pine needles will be of considerable help in retaining moisture, as well as in reducing weed growth. Mulch will also reduce fluctuations in soil temperature during the winter which, in turn, will reduce the incidence of crown rot.

Trickle or drip irrigation is preferable to sprinkler irrigation, as it reduces the possibility of foliage diseases.

These systems may need to be run for two or more hours to wet the soil to the required depth of 1 foot.

Asparagus weed control

Weeds must be controlled if asparagus is to perform well. They can be pulled or removed with a hoe, cultivator or rototiller, but cultivation must be shallow to avoid damage to the asparagus roots. Organic mulches such as grass clippings, straw or leaves help control weeds, as well as retaining moisture. Apply a 2- or 3-inch layer in the fall after the foliage dies. This will reduce weeds throughout the year. The asparagus spears will emerge through the mulch in the spring.

Do not use table salt or other salts to control weeds in asparagus. They build up in the soil and reduce yields, as well as shortening the lifespan of the asparagus planting.

Asparagus disease control

Asparagus is subject to asparagus rust and fusarium root or crown rot.

Rust appears as small, reddish-yellow spots on the stems near the ground. Spores may be scattered by the wind and, if sufficient moisture is present, all the plants may be infected. Fusarium rot attacks feeder rootlets, main storage roots and plant crowns. It weakens and eventually kills plants. It rarely produces wilt symptoms, except on young shoots of seedlings. The fungus builds up in the soil and persists for many years. Asparagus spears infected with fusarium may show a brown surface discoloration. The varieties in this publication have some tolerance to fusarium. In addition, gardeners should always plant asparagus in well-drained soil, avoid replanting in old asparagus beds and keep crowns cool during the winter by using organic mulches.

Asparagus insect control

Asparagus beetles are the main insect attacking asparagus. They are 1/4 inch long, blackish beetles with yellow to- orange markings on their wings. They over winter as adults in trash around the garden and in old asparagus stalks. The adults feed on young spears and attach tiny, black eggs to both spears and foliage. Larva hatches from the eggs and feed on the plant. In severe infestations, most of the foliage may be damaged.

Begin control of asparagus beetles by removing old foliage as soon as it is killed by freezing weather. Burn this residue or turn it under. Asparagus beetles are easily killed
by available home garden chemicals.

Asparagus harvesting

Asparagus should not be harvested the year it is planted. A light harvest of about two weeks the second year will increase the number of buds on the crowns and result in subsequent higher yields. Harvest for about four weeks the third year and six to eight weeks thereafter.

Harvest by snapping the spears off at the ground level when they are 6 to 10 inches tall. This will result in less damage to un emerged spears and less chance of introducing disease into the plant than the traditional harvesting method of cutting the spears below the ground level. It is desirable to harvest at least every other day during cool weather and every day during warm weather to prevent spears from growing too tall. Too many spindly spears indicate weak storage roots. Cease harvest for the season if too many spindly spears appear. Additional fertilizer may be needed and the harvest season may need to be shortened in future years.

Asparagus storage
It's best to cool your C as rapidly as possible once you've harvest it (harvesting in the morning is also desirable if possible). An ice-water bath is an effective way to cool asparagus rapidly. Fill your sink with water and ice; when you've picked your asparagus, place it in the ice-cold water to rapidly cool it. After cooling your asparagus, refrigerate it; it will keep for 2 to 3 weeks at 35° to 40°F. It goes bad quickly over 40°F. Asparagus can be blanched and frozen, canned, and pickled. Jenny pickles asparagus and it's a family favourite during the holiday season.

Beets and Chard

Growing beets and chard as food is traceable to the Mediterranean as far back as 2000 B.C.

In the 1800's, agricultural scientists in Germany developed the sugar beet. Growing white-coloured sugar beets has become a primary source of white sugar (sucrose), along with sugar cane.

The primary beets grown in gardens for eating are known as "garden" beats. Eastern Europeans are especially fond of growing beets for "borsch," a beet-based soup. Garden beets are close relatives to Spinach.

Beets and chard characteristics

Beets and chard are a root crop with edible tops. When the plants are young and the leaves are tender, these beet greens are excellent in salads. As the plant grows older, the greens can be cooked as you would spinach. Their roots are even more versatile. They can be cooked fresh from the garden, you can store them in a cool place for winter use, you can make pickled beets or they are good for canning.

Beets and chard climatic requirements
Even though they are somewhat tolerant of heat, they will do best in cool climates, and they can also withstand cold weather short of severe freezing. Beets and chard will mature quickly, between 55 to 70 days; they don't need much room and only require a minimum of care. There is one caution however - they won't do very well in extremely acid soil.

Beets and chard best location
Planting beets and chard where beans grew the previous year will benefit the plants. All beans enrich the soil with nitrogen-fixed form the air, improving the conditions for whatever crop you plant after the beans are finished.

Beets do not grow well near walnut trees; garlic improves growth and flavor of beet plants; rather than planting invasive mints around beets use your mint clippings as mulch.

Radishes are a deterrent against cucumber beetles and rust flies, and leaf miners; sage deters unwanted pests and benefits each other in garden; runner or pole beans and beets stunt each other's growth; beets are closely related to Swiss chard and spinach. Avoid following these crops in rotation.

Beets and chard soil
Like any root crop, you'll get the best results planting in soil that is root and rock free. Loose soil is critical for proper development of the roots. If all you have is rocky soil, sift the planting area a minimum of 6 "down.

Deeply till the soil, and then smooth the surface in order to prepare a good seed-bed. If your soil is heavy clay, hard, or alkaline, mix in an inch or so of compost.

The optimum pH range is between 6 and 6.5. Beets do not grow well in high acidic soils (a pH lower than 6).

Beets and chard varieties

Given properly prepared soil, beets and chard can be grown practically anywhere in America that plants will grow. I've never tried a variety of either that wasn't delicious, though you'll find over time that certain varieties may grow a little better or taste a little better in your specific location. I'll give you a list of my favourite varieties, and I think you'll find them well suited, but please don't limit yourself to just my suggestions.

- **Beets:** Bull's Blood, Early Wonder, Cylindra, Detroit Dark Red
- **Chard:** Ruby Red, Rainbow (aka five-color silverbeet), Fordhook Giant

Beets and chard fertilizer and lime

To prepare your soil for planting, you need to spade it well, approximately 8 inches in depth, and rake out any stones. If you have acid soil, work in some lime at least a week before planting. Wood ashes, which contain lime and potash, are a good source for reducing acidity. Before you begin to sow, apply a 5-10-5 fertilizer, roughly 1/2 pound for 25 feet of row.

Beets and chard planting and spacing

For continuous harvest, make successive planting every two week into early summer or up to soil temperatures of 65°F. Beets grow best in soil temperatures of 60° to 65°F. For a fall harvest, begin planting again 8 weeks before your first expected frost date.

Planting beets and chard consecutively rather than one big crop will provide smaller, more tender beets throughout the season.

If you live in a mild winter area, beets can be planted in the fall with consecutive plantings throughout winter and into spring.

The seeded rows of beets should be spaced at least 14 inches apart, and the furrows should be about 1/2 inch deep. Sow the seeds, which are clusters of three or four seeds to a casing, at 1-inch intervals. The plants will come up in little clumps, and then you should thin them to one plant per inch when they reach about 2 inches tall. After 4 inches, thin down to four to six plants per foot.

For mid-summer plantings, the furrows should be about an inch deep; to reach the moisture in the soil, and then cover the seeds with leaf mould, or some other type of material that won't form a crust, water needs to run through the material.

Beets and chard irrigation

Speedy growth and timely harvesting are key factors to tender, juicy beets. Slow growth comes from too little water, too fe w nutrients, or a weed infestation; this will also cause the roots to be tough and weedy. If fertilization was done before planting, you only need repeat it once again before harvesting. When seedlings are about 3 inches high, scatter some 5-10-5 fertilizer along each side of the row - roughly 5 ounces for every 10 feet. Then cover with a light mulch, straw, sawdust, or lawn clippings, to help conserve moisture and keep the weeds to a minimum. If the weeds persist, remove from each row by hand, and shallowly hoe between the rows so as not to injure the roots of the beets. Don't forget to water on a regular basis.

Beets and chard weed control

Weed control is vital in establishment when growing beets, especially in the early stages. Hand weed, being careful not to disturb or damage beet roots. The root crops grow slowly for the first few weeks after planting and cannot successfully compete with weeds. Frequent, shallow cultivation will control the weeds and keep the surface of the soil loose.

The roots of the root crops are very close to the surface of the soil, so it is important not to cultivate too deeply. Cultivate just deeply enough to cut the weeds off below the surface. Deep cultivation after the weeds are large damages the beet roots.

Beets and chard disease control

If you sow your beets too early they may "bolt", that is they will run to seed rather than form edible roots, only if the temperature remains below 40 degrees F. for a number of weeks. If this should happen, pick the leaves and use them for salad greens and re-sow the row. If you have already limed the soil, and the leaves become stunted or yellowish, you may have phosphorus deficiency. If this is the case, add fertilizer, superphosphate or a covering of bone meal.

Beets and chard insect control

Beets and chard are prey to few pests, particularly where the winter freeze kills bugs and larvae in the soil. In warmer areas beets may be attacked by tiny yellow leaf miners, which can be controlled with an organic pesticide.

Leaf spots may develop if you grow the beets in the exact same spot you planted them the year before. This fungus can be destroyed by spraying with a fungicide.

If the roots develop black areas, which is an indication the soil may be deficient in boron. This can be added to the soil by mixing 1/4 teaspoon of household borax with 12 gallons of water. This mixture can be sprinkled where you are going to plant your future beet crop.

Beets and chard harvesting

Beets and chard can be harvested at any stage of development, from the thinning to the fully mature stage at about 2 inches in diameter. As the roots get larger they tend to get more fibrous.

Beets must be harvested before the ground freezes in the fall. Hand pull by pushing the root to the side and pulling it out of the ground. Remove as much dirt as possible. Do not wash unless using immediately. Cut or twist off the tops of the beets 1" above the root to prevent staining (or bleeding) during cooking. If you are removing the entire crop at one time, it may be helpful to use a spading fork to loosen the soil next to the plants before pulling them. Harvest your thinnings by cooking up the small beets and using the chard in salads.

For a fall harvest, pull up your beet crop after a hard frost. Beets and chard harvested in fall have stronger colors than spring-planted beets and usually have higher sugar levels

Beets and chard storage

Beets and chard can be stored in a Ziploc bag in your refrigerator for several weeks. They also store well in a root cellar or cool, dark area packed in peat, sand or sawdust with moderate to high humidity for 2-4 months. Cut tops ½ "from the root when storing.

Harvested beets also may be stored in a pit in the ground covered with enough straw to keep from freezing. Ideal storage temperature for beets is 32°F with 95 percent humidity. Do not allow the roots to freeze.

Beets and chard can be frozen, canned or pickled and dried beets yield fairly good results.

Freezing magnifies imperfections and woodiness in over mature beets. For freezing, select deep, uniformly-red, tender, young beets. Canning Beets with a diameter of 1 to 2 inches are preferred for whole packs. Avoid canning beets more than 3 inches in diameter as they are often tough and fibrous.

Cabbage, Broccoli, and Cauliflower

Cabbage, broccoli, and cauliflower are from the Brassicaceae or Cruciferae family under the group of Brassica oleracea Capita. It was local to the Mediterranean region coming from a leafy mustard herb. The ancient Romans and Greeks have used the vegetables to prepare some forms of medicine. They have extracted white juice from newly picked these plants and used it to relieve painful or Irritated eyes. The Romans and ancient Egyptians also took the concoction to prevent intoxication.

"Caboche" is believed to be the root of the English name of cabbage. It is derived from the Normanno Picard word which means "head". Cabbage, broccoli, and cauliflower has proven itself to be one of the most useful vegetables in history. It has earned for itself a very high position in the list of nutritious foods.

Cabbage, broccoli, and cauliflower characteristics

These are annual plants that mature in about 90 days. These plants prefer well drained rich soil although you have to keep the plants wet when you water them. It may not be a really popular plant among many gardeners but those who love it would want to know how to grow cabbages will have to put in a little work so you can get a good harvest.

Cabbage, broccoli, and cauliflower climatic requirements
Those who live in the eastern states will have more options when to grow these veggies. It is typical for people who live in these areas to grow them during fall to spring. However, those who live in colder climates still have the opportunity to grow these vegetables. It is best that those who live in colder places to plant their cabbages in the middle of summer.

Cabbage, broccoli, and cauliflower best location
Full sun and very fertile, well drained soil.

Cabbage, broccoli, and cauliflower soil
All members of the brassica family (such as cabbage, broccoli, cauliflower, collards, kale, and Brussels sprouts to name a few) are big consumers of soil nutrients. Add plenty of well-rotted manure and compost to the soil before planting. Cabbage plants prefer a liberal, balanced amount of nitrogen, potassium, and phosphorus. Many problems with cabbage are avoided when the pH level is right around 7.2. If your soil pH is low, adding lime will bring it up.

Cabbage, broccoli, and cauliflower varieties
Cabbage comes in many forms. It is often classified according to its shape and maturity. Green cabbages are the most common. Red cabbages are very rich in nutrition and are often thinly shredded to prepare delicious fresh salads. More delicate forms like the Bok Choy, a Chinese variety, can also be found.

My favourite varieties of broccoli are Atlantic and Waltham 29. Both of these varieties produce a lot of side shoots once the main head is cut and have a classic broccoli taste. I usually plant Atlantic in the spring and Waltham 29 in the fall. I've had best results in my area with the Early Snowball variety of cauliflower. Cauliflower is vulnerable to earwigs, and we have a lot of them! A quick-growing cauliflower gives the best odds of a harvest with minimal insect damage.

The foregoing is simply my current preferences and will necessarily reflect my own tastes as well as climate and soil. These are excellent varieties for starting your exploration, but you shouldn't limit yourself.

Cabbage, broccoli, and cauliflower fertilizer and lime

The first step on how to grow these vegetables is to prepare your garden soil. It should be made rich and fertile, which basically means you have to add fertilizer to your garden soil. Blend in compost before transplanting your seedlings. Use fertilizers only once a month. Though they grow well where it is warmer, you should plant them with about 50% shade. Use your shade cloth to achieve this effect. A good idea is to have them start on flats. This is an important point to remember on how to grow cabbages. Transplant the young cabbage plants you bought in order to keep the first real leaves above the soil.

Cabbage, broccoli, and cauliflower planting and spacing

All members of the brassica family grow great in cool temperatures with optimal temperatures ranging from 45 to 75 degrees. Hot weather is not ideal for growing vegetables. You may plant your seeds indoors a month or so before your last frost and then transplant your seedlings to you garden. The seedlings will probably be about 3 to 4 inches tall at that time and transplanting them is very easy to do.

When planting them, be sure to space them out a good bit so they will have plenty of space to grow.

Space them 12-18" apart with 2-3' between rows to allow for spreading roots. Wider spacing provides space for larger heads to develop but young, smaller headed cabbages are more tender and flavourful. To get the best of both worlds, space vegetables 12" apart and harvest every other one when about the size of a softball for fresh eating, leaving the rest to fully mature for storage.

Cabbage, broccoli, and cauliflower irrigation
Keep moisture levels even and soil well drained throughout the growing season. Waterlogged soil will decrease the quality of cabbage. Sufficient amounts of organic matter are necessary due to its ability to either hold, or drain excess moisture.

Cabbage, broccoli, and cauliflower weed control
Young plants do not fare well if they are competing for space with weeds; it will slow their growth. Weeding is critical for plant development but be extremely cautious of the cabbage's shallow, dense root system which can be easily damaged by using garden tools.

If a weed is growing too close to the root system, clip it at ground level; this will avoid damaging the plants root system. Once the heads begin to form, hand weeding is recommended. Applying a layer of mulch will help keep the weeds under control and help maintain even moisture levels.

Cabbage, broccoli, and cauliflower disease control
Transplant the young plants you bought in order to keep the first real leaves above the soil. Keep plants about six inches away from each other. Remember to pack the soil so the roots will be covered completely. Once you have a row of young cabbages planted you should protect them from the common pests that plague them. Cover your rows of vegetables with lightweight row covers.

Cabbage, broccoli, and cauliflower insect control
There are a few things you can do to keep growing plants from being attacked by pests:
• Overhead watering will help detach insects from the plants.
• Controlling nitrogen levels will keep the aphid numbers down; high levels of nitrogen have been shown to increase aphid population.
• Using compost or straw mulches will significantly reduce the amount of fly larvae hatched directly into the soil. It also serves as a habitat for ground and rove beetles, predators of the plants maggot.
• Floating row covers used during the critical period after the plants emerges or right after transplanting will prevent larvae hatchings.
Clubroot (a fungus that attacks the roots) that can be controlled by keeping soil pH at 7.2. If pH levels drop below that, liming is recommended.

Cabbage, broccoli, and cauliflower harvesting
Plants heads can be harvested when the head becomes firm. For the most tender, flavourful heads, harvest when the size of a softball; what they are lacking in size these small heads will make up in flavour. When harvested at this size, the plant will often produce a second head.
Allow growing plants heads to mature for the highest yields. (See 'Spacing' for harvesting tips)
Be sure to keep an eye on the weather forecast. Rain may cause fully-ripened plants heads to split. If this happens, you have a short time in which to harvest your cabbage or they'll begin to rot.
At the harvest, cut as close to the head as possible and this will allow for more small heads to grow. These can grow 2 or more inches and are quite tasty.

Cabbage, broccoli, and cauliflower storage
Bruised heads shorten storage life. Red plants stores better than green. Early varieties do not store well.

For late varieties: pull whole plant, roots intact rather than cutting. Remove outer and damaged leaves. Place on shelves or in a cellar wrapped in newspaper.

Corn.

Throughout much of the world, corn is known as Maize (sounds like mays). The Aztecs and Mayans (S. America) were growing corn well before it made its way to Europe in the 15th century.

In N. America, commercial farmers favour growing corn over any other crop by around double.

One of the oldest forms of corn is popcorn. Popcorn found in New Mexico and has been dated to around 3600 B.C.

Sweet corn is eaten as a vegetable most often (think "corn-on-the-cob), while Field Corn is typically what is grown commercially for animal feed and ethanol.

Corn characteristics

Sweet corn is a crop that can be classified into three groups, normal sugary or standard, sugar enhanced, and supersweet. All three groups have their own unique characteristics and qualities, along with growing conditions.

Corn climatic requirements

Corn will grow best during summer as it prefers warm weather. Try to plant your corn about 14 days before the last frost and to stop your various varieties of corn form cross-pollinating each other, stagger your plantings about a week apart. This will also make harvesting a lot easier as the corn will not be ready all at the same time.

Corn best location

Plant your corn in full sun with some protection from the wind if possible. Plant corn in the North side of the garden so the tall corn plants won't shade out the rest of your garden.

Alternately, if you have plants that need partial shade during the hotter parts of the summer, position your corn to protect those crops from too much sun.

Corn is a heavy nitrogen feeder, so it will thrive in an area where nitrogen-fixing plants such as beans, peas, clover, or alfalfa grew the previous season.

Corn soil

Rich soil with good drainage such as sandy loam is ideal for planting corn. If you do not have sandy loam, remedy this by adding plenty of compost to your soil prior to planting corn. For the best soil pH for growing corn, your soil needs to measure about 6.8 on the pH scale.

Corn varieties

Normal sugary, is the traditional flavor of corn and can be either a hybrid or open-pollinated. The normal sweet corn cultivars that have been grown for years contain the sugary "su" gene that produces an average amount of sugar and is responsible for the kernels sweetness and creamy texture. The only downside to this cultivar of corn is that it's sugar changes over to starch fairly quickly, leaving them best suited to be picked and either processed or eaten in a short period of time after harvested.

Sugar enhanced varieties of corn are sweeter than the normal sugary variety, and contain a sugar enhancing gene "se" that raises the sugar content significantly while still retaining the tenderness and the creamy texture of the normal varieties. The SE varieties are the home gardeners gourmet corn of choice due to there noticeable outstanding taste, tenderness and texture. If you decide to plant this variety of corn along with the normal sugary varieties, there is no isolation necessary between these two crops.

Supersweet corn varieties are a little more of a challenge to grow for the home gardener. They are a crop that cross-pollination is a concern and should be isolated from any other corn type. The kernels of this extra sweet variety have a crispy, tough skin texture, not the creamy texture of the other varieties. This texture isn't really noticeable if the corn on the cob is eaten fresh, but does affect the quality of frozen or canned corn. Unless your corn needs to be stored, shipped or harvested by mechanical methods, this isn't really the best choice for the home gardener.

Corn fertilizer and lime

The Indians plant a kernel of corn on top of a dead fish and while most people think that this is a myth the nitrogen in decaying fish actually provides the corn with the food it needs to grow. This does not mean that you will have to go and buy a bulk load of fish for your corn. Rather provide it with a steady supply of good organic fertilizer like alfalfa meal or dried animal dung during the growth period and your corn will be just as tasty as the ones that were planted with the fish.

Corn planting and spacing

If this is the first time you will attempt to grow corn you will need to ideally turn the soil during in autumn so that you can plant your corn during spring. You can however, turn the soil and plant the corn in spring and end up with a fairly good harvest.

Planting Basics: seed depth: approx. 2" (3" in sandy soil) - seed spacing: 3" to 4" (we like to over-plant and thin our corn to 8" to 12" apart) - row width: 30"to 36" (I like to plant rows 36" apart so I can get my Troybilt Horse Tiller "Attiller the Hun" between the rows).

It's important not to crowd your plants as the corn ears will be smaller (or not form at all). Corn is wind-pollinated, so plant four or more short rows of sweet corn side-by-side rather than one or two long rows. This will help insure good pollination and ear development. Inadequate pollination results in poorly-filled ears.

Corn irrigation

Although corn is a warm-weather crop, a lack of water at critical periods can seriously affect development of the ears and reduce yield. If rainfall is sparse, be sure to water your crop thoroughly (1 to 1.5 inches per week) when the tassels emerge, and when the ears and silk appears.

Push your finger into the soil to check for moisture. If you feel the soil dry more than 1" down, the plants need watered. Sandy soils may require more frequent watering. The roots of the Corn plant are located close to the stalks. It is also a very shallow root system, therefore when watering; place the water source near the base of each stalk to be sure the roots are able to absorb the water.

Corn weed control

Weeds are a problem almost immediately after planting. Mulching right after planting will help to keep weeds down, but is really only practical on a small plot. Mulch between the rows, but mulch between plants only when they reach six to eight inches in height. If you are cultivating by hand, rake your plot about three days after planting to get weeds that might be germinating. On a larger plot, use a rotary hoe or spike-tooth harrow with the teeth set very shallow. When the corn gets high enough for you to see rows easily across the field or garden, begin cultivating with shovel cultivators or with a tiller Be careful not to bury the plants with clumps of dirt. As the corn grows higher, you can be less careful about cultivating since you won't have to worry so much about burying the plants.

Corn disease control

If you have grown corn before, do not plant it in the same spot as the previous year as this can encourage pest and disease problems to recur. Corn is also a heavier feeder and takes a lot of nutrients out of the soil. By rotating your planting spots you will give your soil a chance to recover. The seeds should ideally be planted in a seedbed which is 8 to 10 inches deep.

Corn insect control

The three primary pests that threaten to destroy your crop are animals, insects and diseases. Make sure you examine your corn plants at regular intervals for danger of infestation. Corn earworms are also pests that you need to watch out for and they usually have an affinity for sweet corn that they attack consistently every year.

First, to keep the earworms from entering the trip of the husk, you can wrap a rubber band around the tip of the ear or attach a clothespin after the corn silk appears. This method will go a long way in minimizing the damage.

Secondly, you can protect your corn plants by spraying an insecticide called BT or Bacilulus Thuringiensis that contains a particular bacterium which will affect and attack only the larvae of the corn invader.

Corn harvesting

Check your stalks when the silks are brown and damp by poking a fingernail into a kernel - it's ready when the liquid that squirts out is milky. This stage occurs about 18 to 24 days after the appearance of the first silk strands. Sweet corn remains in the milk stage less than a week.

Signs that indicate the corn is ready for harvest are: drying and browning of the silks, fullness of the tip kernels, and firmness of the un-husked ears.

To harvest your corn, snap off the ears by hand with a quick but firm downward push, twist and pull. Hold the stalk with the other hand just above where the ear attaches to the stalk to prevent it from breaking.

Corn storage

For preservation of flavour and sugar content corn must be brought to 40°F within 1 hour from harvest or the sugars quickly begin to turn to starch. The quickest way to accomplish this is to give the corn an ice bath.

Corn only preserves well for about 1 week in the refrigerator; after picking, use the sweet corn immediately for fresh eating, canning, freezing, or dehydrating. In my opinion, freezing sweet corn is the best way to preserve the taste of corn.

Potatoes

Potatoes are one of the widely grown vegetables in the whole world. Potatoes do not start as seeds. They are planted from tubers. It is also sensitive to many diseases. It is important to know the right ways how to grow potatoes. You can buy tubers of potatoes from centres for gardening. You should buy tubers that are certified by the government. These tubers are also called seed potatoes.

Potatoes characteristics

One of the easiest vegetables to grow is the potato. Whether you grow a main crop to keep you in roasties all though the winter or deliciously sweet salad potatoes to enjoy during the summer, the principles of growing them are the same. Planted in the ground, potatoes do take up a lot of room on your vegetable garden, but you can just as easily grow them in containers or large bags. Here is a short guide to planting and growing potatoes in your garden.

Potatoes climatic requirements

Do not plant potatoes too early, while the ground is still icy. If the ground is too cold and wet, the seed potatoes will delay sprouting until the growing conditions are more favourable. This is usually in early March to late April, depending on the climate. Potatoes do tolerate cool soil and a light frost, but not much growth will take place until the soil warms up a bit.

Potatoes best location

Potatoes should be planted in an area that receives at least six hours of full sunlight daily.

If you're converting lawn to garden area, it is best to avoid planting potatoes in the new garden area for at least the first year as they may be assaulted by grubworms.

Potatoes prefer well-drained soil with moderate quantities of organic matter and sand.

Potatoes soil

Potatoes grow best if the pH level of your soil is around 4.8 to 5.5; they'll usually do OK even up to 6.5, although they may have more scabbing.

If your soil has a pH above 6.0, you can purchase potato varieties that are scab-resistant.

Potatoes require a decent amount of potassium and phosphate which is typical of root crops.

Potatoes varieties

Russet Potatoes – This potato is slender, oval shaped with a rough brown skin and lots of eyes. They have a mealy texture when cooked and cooked russets will start to fall apart when cut due to the low moisture and high starch content. This variety of potato easily absorbs butter, dressings and sauces. They are best used for baking, frying and mashing.

White, Red and Yellow Potatoes – These potatoes are round and keep their shape when cooked. Due to their high moisture and low starch content, they have a firmer texture and won't fall apart when cut after cooking; they're also slow to absorb butter, dressings and sauces. These potatoes are best for boiling, steaming and roasting. They are also excellent creamed or scalloped and in salads. Yellow and red potatoes may be mashed, but they will not be as fluffy as russet potatoes.

New Potatoes – Freshly harvested and marketed during the late winter or early spring, new potatoes are tiny to small potatoes of any variety. Their skin is tender and they do not need to be peeled. When cooked, they have a firm, waxy texture. New potatoes are best when used soon after harvest and prepared by boiling, steaming or roasting.

Potatoes fertilizer and lime

Mix a general fertilizer on the soil 2 weeks before the potato planting season. Do not add lime, the newly grown potatoes prefer slightly acidic soils with pH of just under 6. Seasoned gardeners who know how to grow potatoes normally don't plant them in the same ground in successive years but leave 2-3 seasons before planting potatoes again. This technique prevents the build-up of diseases and which can hinder the crop growth drastically.

Potatoes planting and spacing

In Northern areas, you can begin planting and growing seed potatoes directly in the garden 14-21 days before the last frost date.

Potatoes can withstand a light frost, and even if the plants wilt and turn black with a heavier frost, the plants will come back (this happened to us last year).

You can begin growing most varieties of potatoes in late March or April; if you plant too early in the spring you run the risk of your seed potatoes rotting before they grow.

If you've prepared your trench well, you should have loose, well-drained soil to plant your potatoes in; place one of your cut seed potatoes every 10 to 12 inches.

Potatoes irrigation

Potato crops should always get enough sunlight and water each day while growing. To get the best results, wet up the potatoes very early in the morning so they get time to absorb the water and dry throughout the day. This is supposed to increase the chance of maintaining a very successful crop.

Potatoes weed control

Once the potatoes shoot out vines, they effectively squelch weeds. If you don't use any form of mulch, you'll need to hand pull competing weeds early in the season.

Potatoes disease control

Because potatoes are so prone to several serious diseases, make sure that you buy certified seeds that are germ free that have been chosen to give you the best results with the most chance of having a successful harvest. These seeds can be found at most quality nurseries and garden centers. Don't utilize the potatoes from in the supermarket because your seed even if they look healthy but they are not appropriate for growing potatoes.

Potatoes insect control

Another potential problem with potatoes is the Colorado potato beetle. The larvae and adult beetles will feed on the potato foliage, and a heavy infestation can damage the foliage enough to reduce your harvest considerably. Watch for the beetle's yellow eggs on the undersides of leaves and crush the clusters whenever you see them. Larvae are a deep orange colour with a row of black spots on both sides, while the adults are a paler orange with black stripes on the body and black spots on the head. The larvae and adults can be picked off the leaves and crushed if there are only a few. An infestation can also be controlled with Bacillus thuringiensis, or Bt. Bt is an organic control that is very safe to use. Look for Bt that is specifically for potato beetles. It is sold in many garden catalogues and garden centres.

Potatoes harvesting

You can begin to harvest "new potatoes" when potato plants are still green - we usually wait until the plant is flowering.

Harvest your potatoes after most of the vines have died, before the soil temperature drops below 40°F, causing the starches to turn to sugar (makes potatoes lose their flavor).

Harvest just after a light frost and before the heavy frosts begin in the fall; if you can, wait a couple of weeks to let the potato skins harden.

Place shovel about a foot away from the main potato vine and dig straight down; pull back on your shovel...you should pop up a potato or two or three...repeat on the opposite side and continue down the row this way.

Be careful not to accidentally skin the potatoes as it will affect their long-range storability.

Don't wash your potatoes until you're ready to use them.

Potatoes storage

Store potatoes for a couple of weeks in a cool, dry area at about 55° to 60°F, then store them in a very cool, dark place - 40° to 45°F at 90% Humidity - through the winter.

The best practice for storing tomatoes is to layer newspaper between the layers of potatoes in a wooden box if you're able to buy or build them.

We dug a 4' x 6' x 54" deep hole, lined it with a plywood box, and put our root crops in the bottom, covered them with about 18" of barley straw, and covered the hole with an old 3/4" sheet of plywood. It stays right about 40°F all winter in our "root cellar."

Peppers.

If you're growing peppers this year in your garden, it's best to note a couple basic facts. First, whether you're growing sweet peppers (also referred to as bell peppers) or if you're growing hot peppers, the growing instructions are essentially the same for either type of pepper.

Second, if you're growing your peppers from seed, you'll have way more variety choices than if you purchase pepper starts from a garden centre.

Peppers characteristics

The pepper and the numerous relatives of its extended family - green, red, orange, yellow, small and spicy, large and sweet - are one of the characteristic ingredients of Spanish cooking. They can be dried and ground into powder to produce pimentón, a unique Spanish flavouring used in a variety of dishes - including paella. They can be roasted or preserved whole by various methods: in vinegar or brine, or peeled and bottled in their own juices. And of course, they can be eaten fresh, as an ingredient in one of countless Spanish recipes or summer salads all around the world. Stuffed whole peppers are common in many cuisines.

Peppers climatic requirements
When planting peppers in Northern climates it's a very good idea to get an early start, so we typically plant our peppers indoors under grow lights around 2 months before our last frost. This will produce better results due to the longer growing season for your peppers.
It's the best practice to grow your peppers in an area with full sun. Shade or partial shade will hurt your plants' productivity as well as the flavour of your peppers.

Peppers best location
Peppers enjoy the same kind of growing conditions as tomatoes, so they make ideal companions. If you do decide to grow both, make sure you grow the peppers on the sunny side of the greenhouse so they are not shaded by the faster growing and much taller tomato plants. Many modern cucumbers produce only female flowers, but some greenhouse varieties produce both male and female blooms, the female flowers have a small embryo fruit behind the petals. Pinch out male flowers before they have a chance to pollinate the female ones, because the resulting cucumbers will taste bitter.

Peppers soil

Add plenty of compost to your soil. Manure may also be necessary but be careful not to create excessive nitrogen. Peppers are sensitive and the resulting factor will be outstanding foliage with less than normal production in fruit.

Peppers varieties

Your garden just wouldn't be complete without the addition of delicious sweet bell peppers. Peppers are a very common staple in kitchens and there are varieties to choose from. You have your choice of red, yellow, green, and orange, as well as various hot peppers as well. Growing Peppers is easy to do and they'll grow without a great deal of effort. Not to mention how peppers will add delicious flavor to many of your meals.

Peppers fertilizer and lime

You have your seeds ready and your location picked so what's next? The next step is making sure the soil that you're using is well fertilized. If you want perfect growing soil your soil's pH should be around 6.5. A good fertilizer to use is 15-15-15 and you may need to fertilize your soil up to three times a year.

Peppers planting and spacing

Your soil will need to be dug up well with the ideal pH level between 6.7 and 7. Add organic compost to your soil for extra nutrients. Some gardeners apply Epsom salt on top of the soil to add extra magnesium which helps your peppers flourish. Add fertilizer before you sow your seeds as well.

You will more than likely find the adequate space requirements for peppers on the back of your seed packet, however, if you received some pepper seeds from a friend and do not have the packet, just remember to space them out at least twelve inches. Give them plenty of room to grow.

Peppers irrigation

Peppers require full sun and moderate watering. Pick an area of your yard that receives first sunlight in the morning and throughout the day. Water every other day and more often if you experience periods of high heat and dryness.

Peppers weed control
Keep your garden beds weeded to prevent competition from weeds. Further, use an organic mulches, such as manure, to help feed the peppers and prevent weeds.

Peppers disease control
Hand-picking is a good option for pest like the pepper weevil. It feasts on the blossoms causing deformed and discoloured fruit and also for adult pepper maggots that feed on the insides of the fruit causing the pepper to rot and drop off. A floating row cover will also minimize insect populations.

Peppers insect control
Serious infestations call for more drastic measures and can be controlled with Pyrethrins, a natural organic compound derived from the Chrysanthemum that acts as a lethal internal poison to most insects.

Peppers harvesting
As soon as your peppers are ready to use and before they are ripe, pick a few. This will signal the plant to produce more fruit. Pick individual peppers as they ripen through the season.

Peppers storage
We like to store our peppers by either freezing or drying. To freeze, simply wash the peppers, cut up into desired pieces or slices, removing the inner core and seeds. Place in Zip-loc bags and store in the freezer.

To dry, follow the same instructions for washing and cutting then lay pieces, not touching, on dehydrator drying racks. Be certain the meaty pieces are dry all the way through. Drying usually takes 24 hours.

Onions.

One vegetable that is use in almost any curry and forms an indispensable part of the kitchen is onion. Learning how to grow it would come up very handy for anyone. Good news for the aspirants is that it is not difficult adding this excellent vegetable to the garden.

Onions characteristics

Onions can be used as spice, as a vegetable, as a medicine or as ornamentals even. As food or as food ingredient, the onion gives us a lot of health benefits.

Onions have a lot of medicinal effects and these can work whether they are used as food or as medicine preparation. They are used by early settlers to treat various conditions like coughs, asthma, colds and even used to repel insects. In Chinese medicine, they are even used to treat bacterial infections, breathing problems and angina. Onions are also known to help suppress the growth of bacteria in the colon because it encourages the growth of healthy bacteria named bifid bacteria. Thus, it is considered as a good protection against colon tumours.

Onions climatic requirements

You can grow onions from seeds, seedlings, or sets (small bulblets). If you are going to use seeds, begin to grow them inside 4-6 weeks before your last frost and then transplant them into you garden. If you purchase seedlings you can plant them in your garden after your last frost of the season. Sets are probably the best choice for those who are not familiar with growing onions. They tend to be easier to grow and also produce larger onion bulbs.

Onions best location

Selection of right location for growing onion is very important. Places that are exposed to sun well and have good drainage system. Usually having a time span of eight to twelve weeks before the last frost in the location should be perfect for the growth of onion.

Because of their pungency, onions repel most garden pests, and are helpful in protecting other garden plants, too. Onions are good companions for beets, strawberries, tomatoes, and lettuce. But don't grow onions near beans or peas -- onions can seriously stunt their growth.

Onions soil

Onions are cool season plants hence grow well in a loose soil that drains well. Add manure to your soil and fertilize it almost a week before planting the onions. Keep watering the soil occasionally for the steady growth. They need a weed free area, because the presence of weeds around the bulbs hampers its further development. Tilling the soil will not only keep it weed-free, but also help soil retain the moisture.

Onions varieties

Onions belong to allium family and their other family members are chives, leek and garlic. Many varieties of onions are available including bulb onions, multiplier or perennial onions, tree or Egyptian varieties, welsh onions or spring onions, yellow onions and sweet onions. Depending on the variety, onions can be pungent, tangy, mild or sweet. Onions are basically categorized as long and short day varieties. Long day onions are predominantly grown in North America and Europe.

Onions fertilizer and lime

Natural organic fertilizer improves the growth process without exposing the plants to chemicals found in conventional fertilizers. A good organic fertilizer is a natural Mycorrhizal fungi root-builder that makes the roots more susceptible to the existing nutrients found in the soil. Beginners tend over-fertilize their plants by not making use of the NPK content of each kind of fertilizer. NPK stands for the Nitrogen, Phosphorous and Potassium content, and onion plants don't need a high amount, especially if they are started out as bulbs.

Onions planting and spacing

The best time to grow is the spring season usually mid-March to April. Onions fight well against frost and onions can grow well in any climatic conditions. If you are planting the seeds then set them 1 inch apart and 2 cm below the soil. Sow them in rows with 30 cm spacing. When planting sets, leave them around 10 cm apart, then dig a small hole and place the set with neck upwards.

Onions irrigation

Onions require a well-drained, fertile soil which is weed-free at planting time and is kept that way, because the young seedlings are quickly and easily strangled by more vigorous growth. The bulbs are easily damaged, so weed by hand and do not hoe. The onions must be kept evenly watered during the growing period and may be fed with a balanced liquid feed if the spring is cold and they make a slow start.

Onions weed control

Onions need regular weeding to keep the plant healthy. Weeds compete with the onion plants for nutrient consumption, and it is bad for the plant to let a bunch of weeds grow while trying to produce onions. Mulching the soil is an excellent way of keeping the weeds from trying to steal moisture from the onion plant, as well as making a permeable weed barrier.

Onions disease control

Most problems growing peas can be avoided by correct watering and not allowing the soil to become waterlogged.

Powdery mildew can be an issue when the weather warms. Your plants will appear flocked; this white fungal coat will drain all nutrients out of the leaves.

Apply sulphur dust to the foliage early in the season as a preventative.

Onions insect control

Aphids can cause mosaic virus in your peas which causes the plant to yellow and become stunted. Insecticidal soap is effective for this. It will also help with thrips, a tiny dark coloured insect found on the underside of a leaf that distorts and eventually kills the leaf.

The Pea Weevil, a tiny brown beetle with white spots will bore an opening in the blossom and lay eggs in the pods. Eventually they will damage the pea. Crop rotation will help discourage this pest, but if the problems get out of control, use Pyrethrins.

Onions harvesting

Green versions can be harvested when they are still young and green to get milder flavour. Dry onions sometimes become red, white, or yellow in colour. They are harvested once their tops are withered completely and skin becomes dry like a paper.

Onions storage

Onions have long durability. But storing them in a cool dry place will enhance their durability much more. Sometimes the storage is also used for creation of onion sets. These are onion stored from the winter in the storage. Best onion sets would be the ones in the size of marble and those are hard squeezing.

Turnips, Rutabagas and Radishes.

If you are planning on growing these plants, you must know that the radish belongs to the family of Cruciferous; both the roots and leaves of all three are edible and can be cooked in a variety of ways. All three roots are high in vitamin C, folate, thiamine, niacin, and a number of essential minerals including potassium and copper. Their omega-3 to omega-6 fat ratio is 3:1, and they are a substantial source of cardio-protective dietary fiber.

Turnips, rutabagas and radishes characteristics

Growing radishes was pioneered before the Roman empire; the name "radish" derived from "radix," the Latin word for "root" (the Romans could wield a sword but weren't really clever with names!). Turnips and turnips are close relatives to the radish.

Growing these plants can be a colourful pastime. Colours range from red, pink, and white, to gray-black or yellow radishes, in varying sizes and shapes, the most popular being the red round radish.

Turnips, rutabagas and radishes climatic requirements

Turnips, rutabagas and radishes are one of those vegetables that are fairly easy to grow. In fact it is not necessary to even start them indoors. Regardless of whether you are growing them in a traditional backyard garden or in pots/containers or raised beds, growing them from the seed started outdoors is the best way to go. They can be grown in early spring, after the last frost, or in the autumn before frost sets in and they can germinate in as little as four days in optimal conditions. Do not plant the radish seeds any deeper than 1/2".

Turnips, rutabagas and radishes best location

These plants do well in an area that has at least 6 hours of sun daily, but some shade is OK in the afternoon too.

As mentioned above, radishes prefer cool weather, so some shade is OK if your weather is going to get too warm by harvest time. Turnips, rutabagas and radishes, like most root crops, like well-drained soil. And like most root crops, they like the soil loosened deep enough for them to reach their roots deep into the soil.

Good companions for growing radishes include squash family members, peas, spinach, melons, lettuce, carrots, pole beans, beets, nasturtiums, and chervil.

Turnips, rutabagas and radishes soil

They grow best in a soil with a pH balance in the range of 5.8 to 6.8, although the optimal range is 6.0 to 6.5.

Use a pH tester to check your soil's pH balance. If it's too alkaline (above 6.8), add enough sulphur to bring it down below that level. If it's too acidic (below 5.8), adding lime is the simplest way to raise the pH of your soil quickly.

Before planting them, rototill 2 to 4 inches of well-aged compost into the soil. This should give you most of the nutrients your plants will need for their short growing season. A handful of bone meal also helps every couple of feet down the rows as well.

After tilling your soil, smooth it out, removing rocks, sticks, or other debris in preparation for planting.

Turnips, rutabagas and radishes varieties

The radishes are of two different categories with some popular names like April Cross, Bunny Tail and Red Kings are some of the names for Spring Radishes. Winter Radishes are Black Spanish and White Chinese. Your local agricultural store likely only carries two varieties of turnip at most: Purple Top White Globe and Golden Ball. But if you look in the catalogues of heirloom seed companies, you'll find at least a dozen varieties from which to choose.

Rutabagas are sweeter than turnips, and if your family hasn't developed a taste yet for this family of root vegetables, rutabagas would be a good place to start. Just look through the catalogues and find a variety that looks tasty.

Turnips, rutabagas and radishes fertilizer and lime

A good organic fertilizer will help your plants grow better. The addition of a good organic fertilizer also improves the flavour and increases the "hotness" of your plants. Compost is a good organic fertilizer made of grass clippings, leaves or table scraps. Add compost and turn the soil to mix. To start, sprinkle the seeds over the top of the soil, then scatter a quarter inch of dirt on top of them. The seeds should sprout in three to five days.

Turnips, rutabagas and radishes planting and spacing

As we've discussed previously, radish are a cold-hardy plant and can be planted well before the last frost. We usually plant around the first of May, which is a couple of weeks before the last average frost. Last year we planted around the first of May, then had a surprise late frost around the end of May. The plants were unaffected.

Plant your seeds in the trenches about half an inch to an inch. Backfill the dirt over the seeds and tamp it down lightly to make sure the seeds have contact with as much soil as possible.

Turnips, rutabagas and radishes irrigation

There should be abundance supply of water available to grow plants in addition to soil rich in fertilizers and sunlight. The plants grows well in cold climates.

Turnips, rutabagas and radishes weed control

A light mulching of straw or grass clippings around your plants can help to keep your soil cool and weed free.

Any weeds that you have around your growing vegetables should be carefully pulled or cut off so the radishes don't have to compete for nutrients.

Keeping the surface of the soil lightly cultivated, moist, and weed free will give your veggies the love they need to succeed.

Don't hoe too close or too deep around radishes or any root crop as it will damage the roots and therefore the plants.

Turnips, rutabagas and radishes disease control

Cabbage root maggots are a small-sized white-coloured maggot that tunnels into your radish roots. They come from a fly that looks like a common housefly, but is a bit smaller.

These small maggots are difficult to detect as your plants won't wilt unless it is very hot and your plants are heavily infested, which is not common.

However, the quality of your radish crop will be compromised.

Using row covers in the spring is one solution to keep the flies out, but you'll need to put row covers on before your plants come up.

Turnips, rutabagas and radishes insect control
When insects such as slugs, thrips, fly maggots, aphids, grubs, caterpillars, or mites ingest diatomaceous earth, it punctures their guts and they die from dehydration.
Flea beetles are another garden pest that attack plants, among other garden produce.
These tiny beetles chew holes in leaves and stems of seedling which is when they're most vulnerable, and can weaken or kill the plants.
Row covers are effective if they're completely sealed with dirt or sandbags. Proper nutrition and watering also helps your plants resist flea beetles. Ridding the area of bindweed and wild mustard also helps.

Turnips, rutabagas and radishes harvesting
When your plant roots are around 1 to 1-1/2 inches in diameter, they're ready to harvest. You'll see the "shoulder" of the plant pop up above the soil when they're ready to harvest. If you don't harvest within a day or two, the roots will become pithy, flavourless, and woody.
Spring turnips, rutabagas and radishes are ready to harvest around 3 to 5 weeks after seeding.
Summer plants are varied in size and colour and flavour, but should be harvested young to get the best quality radish.
If they get overripe, their best use is your compost heap to be recycled.
Winter plants need to be harvested at a larger size, and typically are "black," white, or green.

Turnips, rutabagas and radishes storage

Once you've pulled your plants, wash them, cut the stems off about an inch above the root and put in plastic zip lock-type bags and keep in your fridge for up to 2 weeks.

Black winter turnips, rutabagas and radishes will store for up to 4 months at 32°F at 95% humidity in a dark cooler/reefer.

Some gardeners have reported having good luck burying their radishes in the soil of a root cellar for up to a month...haven't tried that one myself as I can only ingest a few radishes a year.

As far as we know, you can't freeze plants successfully, nor do they successfully dehydrate.

Carrots and Parsnips

Just as in the local grocery store, carrots and parsnips range from long, slender and tapered to short, stubby and almost beet-shaped carrots. When you think of all the sizes, carrots are amongst the most versatile home vegetables to grow and you can take your pick of the varieties of seeds - just polish up your green thumb if you can.

Carrots and parsnips characteristics

They are amongst the most popular vegetables to grow in the organic home vegetable garden. Carrots are perhaps so popular because of how easy they are to grow and the versatility they provide in the kitchen. Plants can be used for Juicing, Boiling, Steaming, In Casseroles, Stews and Soups, Grated in Cakes, rissoles, on sandwiches, in salads or simply on their own as delicious carrots and parsnips sticks.

Carrots and parsnips climatic requirements

Plants seeds may be sown outdoors 3 weeks before the last expected frost; and when the soil temperature stays at least 45F during the day. A severe frost can damage young carrots and parsnips.

Germination in carrots is slow, often times taking a month when planted early in cooler temperatures.

In sub-tropical regions plant carrots in fall or winter.

Soil temperatures of 75-80F during the day is optimal and can be accomplished in cooler temperatures by using row covers over the bed to hold in heat.

Carrots and parsnips best location

Carrots and parsnips produce best in full sun but can tolerate light shade. Plant in soil that is mostly free of rocks for best results.

Good companions to carrots are tomatoes, beans, rosemary, cabbage, brussels sprouts, peas, onions, lettuce, radishes, & peppers - all of these all have shorter root systems and do not hinder the formation of the carrot.

Bad companions are celery, dill, and parsnips as their growth are affected by close proximity.

Carrots and parsnips soil

Plants are capable of having a very deep root system (up to 3' feet down).

Loosen the soil in your carrot bed 10-12" down; remove larger rocks and break up clumpy soil. Once the soil is loosened, you can add 12-18" of loose soil on top to form a raised bed if desired.

Mixing fully composted material in will help to loosen the soil, but avoid using fresh manure as the high levels of nitrogen will produce leggy, poor tasting carrots.

Test the pH level in your soil; carrots require a pH between 6.0 - 6.5.

Carrots and parsnips varieties

There are so many carrot varieties available, it can boggle the mind. Varieties in a range of colours, shapes, lengths, and days-to-harvest are available. If you're new at this, pick a single, standard variety; once your skills improve, you'll want to branch out and try something different.
There are very few varieties of parsnips available, and these include Harris Model, Hollow Crown, All American, and Half Long Guernsey. All are longseason varieties that are planted in the spring and harvested after the first fall frost.

Carrots and parsnips fertilizer and lime
If your soil is well prepared and contains ample organic matter you will not need to add any nutrient until the plants have fully emerged. After this a weekly watering with diluted liquid rabbit manure or liquid worm castings will provide most of the required nutrient.

Carrots and parsnips planting and spacing
Plants seeds may be sown outdoors 3 weeks before the last expected frost; and when the soil temperature stays at least 45F during the day. A severe frost can damage young carrots.
Germination in carrots and parsnips are slow, often times taking a month when planted early in cooler temperatures.
Sow your seeds ¼ to 1 inch into your soil and cover back up. You'll want to space your rows 1 -1/2 feet apart. A good rule of thumb is that the more carrots and parsnips you want to grow, the wider you should space

Carrots and parsnips irrigation
The mulch you apply will help provide even moisture levels and minimize weeds. If your soil is dry, gradually water the bed over several days.

Carrots and parsnips weed control
Avoid a sudden heavy watering; this could cause the roots to split.

You should see sprouts in a couple of weeks' time. At this point, you have to be careful with the soil and prevent any weeds from growing in it. Once the seedlings grow enough to grasp, you can begin thinning them. Do not thin the sprouts too much as this can cause encourage weeds to grow.

Carrots and parsnips disease control
When growing carrots and parsnips, your biggest threats are animals such as deer, rabbits, woodchucks and gophers; protecting your garden with fencing is your best option.

Carrots and parsnips insect control
If carrots and parsnips flies (rust flies) are a problem in your area, waiting to plant until after June 1 and harvest before mid-September will avoid the first and second hatching of larvae.
Sage or Black Salsify is also known to repel the carrot fly.

Carrots and parsnips harvesting
Patience is rewarded with sweeter-tasting and crisper plants; carrots and parsnips improve in flavour the longer they have to mature.
You can harvest your carrots as soon as they are big enough to eat or wait until they are fully mature and harvest them all at once for winter storage. If harvesting the entire crop, do so before your first frost in the fall.
Moisten the soil the day before harvesting if needed to soften the soil, making the removal of the carrot easier and less likely to break. The use of a digging bar (inserted a couple inches away from the root and rocking it back and forth) has worked very well for us when trying to remove deep-rooted plants; a spading fork is not recommended as it is more likely to bruise or damage the roots, and a shovel may not reach down far enough causing the carrots and parsnips to break off at the tip.

Carrots and parsnips storage

When storing carrots for the winter, twist off the tops of only the mature, straight, undamaged carrots and line a crate, plastic bucket, or wooden box with newspaper. Layer the carrots (preferably not touching each other) placing newspaper in between layers (sand also works well but is a bit messier to deal with).

Preferably, store in a root cellar or a cool, dark location (such as under the house or in the garage). Ideal storage conditions are 32-40°F and 95% relative humidity.

Tomatoes.

For anyone interested in vegetable gardening, home growing tomatoes is a must. These versatile fruits are fairly labour intensive but highly rewarding. There are hundreds of tasty tomato varieties to choose from, all far superior to anything bought from a supermarket. Whether you enjoy eating them on salads or making them into sauces, there is a tomato variety for everyone.

Tomato plants can be grown outdoors, in greenhouses, in the house or in hanging baskets. Growing tomatoes can be done anywhere; you will just need to give them slightly different care and attention depending on the climate.

Tomatoes characteristics

Today, tomatoes are grown around the world, adapted to a variety of growing conditions with thousands of cultivars. Tomatoes vary in size, colour and flavour, from four-inch diameter beefsteak beauties to the elongated plum tomatoes prized in sauces. Tomatoes rightfully take their place along nutritional super foods, yet in some areas of the world, efforts to mass produce the fruit are causing concern among health experts.

Tomatoes climatic requirements

Tomatoes need a warm and relatively long growing season. In many parts of the country, tomato seeds must be started indoors. Start your seeds 6-8 weeks before the danger of frost is past and garden soil temperature is 60°-70°F.

We used to start our tomatoes indoors earlier than we do now. Here in Eastern Washington State, because we have short growing seasons and long winters, it's hard to resist the gardening bug that infects us in February. Planting too early results in plants growing taller than the grow-lights permit, and a sunny window generally does not provide enough light to prevent spindly growth.

Tomatoes best location

Tomatoes need full sun - make sure your tomato plants get most of the available sun between 7am and 7pm during most of the summer. Tomatoes also need well-drained soil. This can be achieved in raised beds, or by adding well-composted manure and compost to the soil.

We've been successful planting in rocky soil (small stones). The rocks absorb and retain heat and keep the soil warm into the evening.

Good companions with tomatoes are cucumber, lettuce, onion, parsley, basil (repels mosquito and flies), asparagus, bush beans, celery, carrots, mint, chives (promote health), and garlic.

Tomatoes soil

Tomatoes grow best in a slightly acidic soil with a pH of 6.2 to 6.8. Correct amounts of calcium (lime) may be added to the soil to bring the pH level up. One pound of lime per 30 sq. ft. should be sufficient. Lime will also increase your levels of potassium (K). N-P-K Levels: (N)-High (P)-High (K)-High

Tomatoes varieties

There are literally hundreds of tomato varieties out there to choose from but there are only two types of tomato vines; determinate and indeterminate.

Tomatoes fertilizer and lime

Tomato fertilizer is required by the tomato plant if it is to produce large healthy fruit. Regardless of the size owing to the variety of the tomato plant, to be able to pick the best tomatoes of its kind these plants need to be fed on a regular basis so that the plant is able to feed nutrients up through the plant to the growing fruit.

Before rushing out and buying plants or even planting seedlings, the soil where the tomatoes are going to be planted needs preparing with compost and fertilizer. The best idea is to prepare the soil a few days before planting.

Tomatoes planting and spacing

Staked tomatoes are less likely to rot (being off the ground). They produce higher levels of vitamin C due to more sun exposure. Yet, allowing indeterminate (see the addendum at the end of this article that discusses determinate and indeterminate tomato plants) tomato plants to sprawl across the ground will produce more fruit. We made an accidental discovery a few years ago when we were remodeling during planting season. We were lucky to get the plants in at all let alone stake them. To improvise, we just propped football-sized rocks under the tomato clusters of the un-staked plants to keep them off the ground. The result (due to rocks retaining heat) was that we had tomatoes two weeks earlier than anyone else!

The best way we have found to plant tomato starts (and the way our family has done it for three generations) is to dig a trench 6" long and 5"-6" deep for an 8" tall plant. Sprinkle the bottom of each hole with several inches of loose compost (N). Place handful of bone meal (P) and 1 teaspoon Epsom salts (magnesium) which will encourage plant productivity and vitality. Lay the plant down in the hole with only the top leaves showing above the soil level. Be careful not to break the stem when placing it in the hole and bending it upward. You will notice the numerous "hairs" on the stem. Each one of those fine hairs is a potential root and the more of these that can be placed in the ground the stronger root system will develop.

Tomatoes irrigation

Watering amounts should be moderate to high until fruit begins to ripen. During ripening, only small amounts of water should be applied to plants. This promotes better flavor in the tomatoes. Avoid over-head watering. This may cause disease and split the fruit. Try either drip irrigation, or if your garden area is small you can easily apply with a bucket, or watering can. Consistent watering practices also help to maintain plant health and prevent disease which can harm root growth and blossom production.

Tomatoes weed control
One way to cut down on weeds is to mulch, even though some weeds will still get through. Some annual weed seeds that are already in the soil will still poke through and others will fall into the mulch and sprout from there. The roots of perennial weeds that have not been pulled out of the soil will push up through the mulch as well. The good thing about mulch is that even the weeds that do come up will stand out so they can easily be spotted and handpicked. If your garden is in a yard surrounded by a Bermuda lawn, watch out for runners creeping into your tomato garden.

Tomatoes disease control
Many problems with tomatoes can be avoided by maintaining proper pH levels. Applying plenty of organic compost, well-composted manure, and rock minerals (such as lime) listed above, will strengthen your tomato plants against insects and disease. Also, give your plants as much warmth as possible in the spring. One way to accomplish this is with the use of water walls.

If using water walls (I speak from experience, here) be sure to remove them once the plant grows beyond the height of the wall. Otherwise, serious plant breakage may occur when removing the walls.

Tomatoes insect control
Tomato worms – If you see these large green, white-striped caterpillars, pick it off and destroy it. If you are lucky to have chickens to throw this pest to, they will be delighted with the treat.

Spider mites – If you see tiny red spots on undersides of the leaves it is likely spider mites.

Yellow speckling on leaves may indicate your plant is being feasted on by these tiny pests. Knock them off by spraying with water or use a natural, organic insecticidal soap.

Nematodes are tiny, worm – like creatures that attack the plants root system, weakening the plants immunity and stunting growth. Your best natural defence is to rotate your crops every year and buy worm-resistant seed varieties.

If you know what diseases are prevalent in your area, buying seed varieties that are resistant to those diseases will be your best prevention.

Tomatoes harvesting

For immediate usage, tomatoes are best harvested when they turn red (or what ever their ripening color may be) but are still firm on the shoulder of the fruit. Pick ripe fruit daily; do not over ripen. Another method for achieving ripe tomatoes before the frost hits is to "stress" them by cutting the roots about half way around the plant with a shovel. When a frost is predicted, you have two choices...

Option 1: Pick all tomatoes, ripe and unripe. To remove, gently twist or cut off the fruits, holding the vine with your other hand to prevent breaking the vine off. Sort (by ripeness) and place in boxes, one layer thick. Store in a dark, warm area. Even green tomatoes will ripen.

Option 2: Pull your tomato plants up, root and all and hang them up-side down in a dry, warm location such as a garage or basement. The nutrients will continue through the plant and many tomatoes will still ripen. We've had great success with this method.

Tomatoes storage

Tomatoes don't store well but will last several days on the counter, out of direct sunlight. Don't store tomatoes in the fridge, this changes their consistency, making them mushy and less flavorful. Tomatoes are the foundation of many preserved foods. Salsas, pizza and spaghetti sauces, soups, and chopped tomatoes are staples at our home.

My brother freezes his tomatoes whole. The advantage to freezing is that you don't need to blanch your tomatoes; when you thaw the tomatoes; the skins come off as easily as if you'd blanched them. We also discovered that broiling green tomatoes in the oven brings out the flavour and makes for fantastic salsa!

Beans.

Beans are crops that are very productive in the organic garden, along with their rich diversity and nutritional value. Beans being a primal food source, growing and saving heirloom bean varieties add a rewarding feeling of accomplishment.

Beans characteristics

Beans are a member of the legume family, a group of nitrogen fixing plants. This means that they have the unique ability to pull nitrogen from the air and put it into the soil. For this reason, nitrogen-loving plants like tomatoes will usually thrive in spots where bean plants resided the year prior. For extra healthy, vigorous plants, dampen the seeds and coat with nitrogen inoculant before planting. Nitrogen inoculant is a black, grainy substance that aids the plants in their early growth stages.

Beans climatic requirements

To maximize bean plant growth, planting should be done when the temperature drops no lower than 61 degrees F or 16 degrees C. If the temperature dips below this level, your plants may not take root, and may die.

Beans best location
As with all vegetables, beans need a full sun position which gets 6-8 hours of sunlight each day. Beans along with other legumes such as wattles and green manure crops are able to fix nitrogen gas from the atmosphere. There is a symbiotic relationship between the roots and a bacteria called Rhizobium. The nitrogen is stored in the roots in swellings called nodules. The nitrogen is released into the soil when the plant dies and decomposes. Green manure crops such as russel lupins are often grown to about 50cm, then dug into the soil to refresh the nitrogen content of the soil. Beans are a great vegetable to plant after cool season broccoli and cauliflower which use up all the nitrogen present in the soil.

Beans soil
Beans like a pH of between 6-7 and if it is slightly on the alkaline side that is fine with them. Remember to lower your pH you add sulphur and to raise your pH you apply lime. In readiness for your planting beans whether seed or seedling, the soil needs to be open, friable and well drained.

Beans varieties
There are many different types of beans, runner, scarlet, board, French and more. Most beans are annuals. This means that they live between 6-12months. But Runner/Scarlet beans (Phaseolus coccineus are perennial beans and die back over autumn/winter to re-emerge in spring. They are also known as the Seven year bean because that is how long they live. Like all climbing plants, beans need support, even the dwarf varieties. However, the climbing varieties produce more beans than the dwarf (bush) ones.

Beans fertilizer and lime
Fertilize once when the plants start climbing the poles. It's best to use organic methods such as compost, fish emulsion, compost tea, or other organic fertilizers.

Beans planting and spacing
Beans can still be planted as late as June for a decent late-summer harvest. Beans should be about an inch deep and approximately 2-3 inches apart. For rows, plant the beans at the same depth with spacing about 18-24 inches apart. Once the seedlings begin to develop true leaves, the plants can be thinned to six inches apart.

Beans irrigation
Beans with other large seed plants are prone to rotting and the leaves are prone to fungal diseases. It is recommended once you have planted the seeds only water them once. Begin watering again when you see the first leaves appearing. For all your vegetables, I recommend you water them early in the morning. This allows all day for the leaves to dry. If you water them in the evening, the leaves don't dry and mildew develops. Another trick is to water at ground level as overhead watering causes the fungal spores to be splashed up onto the foliage.

Beans weed control
Use mulch for delaying harvest, retaining soil moisture, and weed control. How much and what types can be used? We prefer barley straw as we have a ready and inexpensive supply in our area. You can also use grass clippings or chopped up leaves.

Beans disease control

I have more trouble with diseases, especially powdery mildew. It has a dramatic effect on the plants, causing the beans to taste bitter and horrible. It also reduces the amount of beans you will harvest. To try and control this disease you can mix one level teaspoon of bicarb soda into one litre of water. Add one litre of skim milk and a pinch of Condy's Crystals which you can get from a produce agent (someone that supplies fed etc to horse owners). Spray it on the leaves every two weeks. Remember, only make a small amount, as this type of spray does not keep - the skim milk will go bad and smell disgusting. There is also a good lady bird which can be identified by yellow and black bands. She eats the mildew, so don't kill them.

Beans insect control
I don't have much trouble with pests, except when the seedlings are young. Snails and slugs love young plants, so it important to protect them. You can try picking them off by hand, especially after rain or use a snail trap of beer in a glass jar 1/2 sunken into the ground. They crawl in, get drunk and drown. There is also the finely crushed egg shells circle, that you put around each plant which they hate crawling over. There is a new product for pots, which is a copper strip that you attach around the pot. There is also a spray to repel them with but I haven't tried it.

If you are having trouble with caterpillars, then I suggest using an organic spray called Dipel which the active ingredient is Bacillus thuringiensis. It won't harm you, your children, pets or other beneficial insects. Longlife pyrethrum is also good for sap sucking insects such as white fly and aphids, but also kills caterpillars' earwigs.

Beans harvesting

To tell if the bean are ready to pick they should be about 8-15cm long, a nice colour green and be firm to touch. The best way to tell if they are ready is to harvest one and eat it. Harvesting time varieties from season to season and from temperature zone to temperature zone. It depends on how warm or cold it has been while the flowers and pods are developing.

Beans storage
Beans will remain fresh for about a week if refrigerated.
Once production passes your consumption you may preserve your beans by canning, pickling, or freezing.

Cucumbers.

If you are making the decision to grow foods, the most important next step is to have the best instructions on how to do it properly. As with any process, following a step by step guide is the best way to growing cucumbers successfully.

Cucumber is a widely grown plant which is found in most parts of the world. However, it was originated in India. Growing a cucumber is quite simple and straightforward.

Cucumbers characteristics

There are many types of cucumber, shapes and sizes to choose from and even seedless ones. They are a high yielding crop when planted in a fertile clay soil that has been amended with a good amount of organic matter worked into it, but will do just fine in any garden that has a good soil structure. They don't do well in areas that have standing water.

Cucumbers climatic requirements

Early summer is the best time to plant cucumbers. If you plant them too early and a frost comes through, the plant will be damaged or killed. The ideal temperature for growing cucumbers is around 70 degrees.

Cucumbers best location
Cucumber is a plant that requires plenty of sunshine and heat. Besides, offering plenty of heat you also need to have some extra space. This is mainly due to the reason that cucumbers can grow more than 6 feet long. However, if you don't have adequate amount of space then you can make them stand against a wall. They are a good companion plant for radishes - though why anyone would want either for a companion (on a plate) beats me.

Cucumbers soil
The soil should always be well-fertilized with plenty of humus and compost. No repotting is necessary indoors or out, once seedlings have been placed where they are to grow.

Cucumbers varieties

Cucumber 'Passandra' is an all-female indoor cucumber and highly recommended as a heavy cropper. It produces lots of medium sized slightly ribbed, cylindrical and dark green fruits of 15-18cm long. 'Burpless Tasty Green' is both easy to grow and (as its name suggests) easy on the stomach! It is a very prolific variety, producing tender-skinned, crisp and tasty cucumbers with no bitterness. This variety is also resistant to mildew and high summer temperatures. It grows to about 6ft in height. Cucumber 'Euphya' is another prolific, all-female variety, with good disease resistance. It produces long straight cucumbers with a delicious taste. It is a more hardy variety that will tolerate cooler conditions and can even be grown outside as long as it is placed in a sunny, sheltered position. Cucumber 'Ilas' is a mini variety that is just perfect for those who maybe want to grow cucumbers but don't eat a lot of them. It is a heavy cropper producing crunchy mini cucumbers. It also has high mildew resistance.

Cucumbers fertilizer and lime
Before actual planting of cucumber, you must prepare the soil by incorporating compost and cultivating it thoroughly. Make sure that the soil is loose and have enough drains to avoid water logging. You can also start conditioning your garden soil by introducing organic fertilizer. This will allow the build-up of nutrients on the soil which is very good for cucumber.

Cucumbers planting and spacing
Cucumbers are tropical plant so naturally they need lots of sunlight and space. It would be best to plant cucumbers in early summer. It would not survive even in the mildest frost so you better keep track of the weather when planting cucumbers.
It is of utmost importance to leave some gap between the seedlings. This gap could be of 40cm or more. Make sure the seeds are placed at least 2.5cm deep.

Cucumbers irrigation

When it comes to watering however, as you probably know, the water content in cucumbers are through the roof, so if you want them to be nice and firm and not soggy and splotchy then watering them once a week will do.

Cucumbers weed control

To retain moisture and keep grasses and weeds from growing, you can add mulch to the soil. Tree bark or wood chips and saw dust could be ideal materials for mulching.

Cucumbers disease control

Bacterial infections occur when organisms enter the plant through damages leaves, vines or fruit and can be prevented with careful treatment of the cucumber vines and by keeping pests away from them. Fungal infections happen when airborne spores take root on the surface of the plant and can be prevented with attention to watering habits, pests and, eventually, fungicides.

Cucumbers insect control

Striped and spotted cucumber beetles and squash bugs are very damaging pests of cucurbit crops (such as cucumber, pumpkins, squash, watermelons, and muskmelons). Managing these pests in gardens and small farms can be challenging. Trap cropping and mass trapping, two Integrated Pest Management (IPM) strategies are what you can use to control cucumber beetles and squash bugs with little or no insecticides applied to the cash crop.

Cucumbers harvesting

After 50 days of planting you can harvest your cucumbers. But before that you need to make sure that they are of a suitable size. Another important thing to note here is that their skin colour should be dark green. Yellow coloured cucumbers are not very good. So, you need to harvest them when they are of dark green colour.

Cucumbers storage

Store whole cucumbers in a place with temperatures between 50 and 55 degrees Fahrenheit and with 95% relative humidity. Freshly harvested cucumbers can stay fresh for up to at least 10 days within this temperature range. Cucumbers get cold burns when stored in chilly temperatures below 50 degrees. They spoil too easily and too quickly if stored in warmer temperatures of 60 degrees and above.

Greens

Green gardening is a very rewarding activity. It allows gardeners to work with nature rather than against it and can be enjoyed by anyone & everyone. Those lucky enough to have a large garden can really develop their green gardening skills with big compost heaps, crop rotation, water butts & 'grey water' irrigation systems. Fortunately, green gardening is also possible for those with small gardens or even no garden. A patio or balcony can easily be turned into a fruit or salad bowl. The answer is to grow green using containers.

The good news is that there are many types of fruit and vegetables which can be grown successfully in containers. These range from salad leaves to miniature fruit trees. Using containers you can even 'choose' your soil type by buying compost that is suitable for the plants you wish to grow, rather than putting up with your garden's natural range. But for beginners, or those who have less time to plan and tend their patios/balconies/window boxes etc., some plants really do take to life in a pot more than others. Here are just a few suggestions to help ensure that you get great big juicy rewards for your efforts!

Before we look at these plants in more detail, there are some basic tasks that are essential for good growth. This is because plants in pots are more reliant on you for food & moisture than those in garden beds. To get good crops you will need to:

• water your containers every day (& possibly twice a day in hot weather)

• use a natural, organic plant food to help your plants keep producing all season

This is vital for producing strong, disease resistant plants.

Watering is best done out of the heat of the day so that less is lost through evaporation & more moisture is available to the plants. Adding a layer of mulch to the surface of your compost can also help it to stay moist. Another good idea for hanging baskets & containers is to add some water retaining crystals to the soil when you plant up, this will help to hold water in the compost. For larger tubs & pots, you could cut the bottom off a small plastic bottle & bury it in the compost with the widest part uppermost & at the surface. This allows water to be directed deeper into the compost & nearer to the roots of the plants. Don't forget, even if you don't have room for a water butt, you can still use 'grey' water from your washing up bowl or bath to water your plants.

Green gardening generally relies on improving soil condition and structure to add nutrients and encourage strong growth. This is more difficult to achieve with container gardening, so additional nutrients may be required. Organic plant foods are available from a wide variety of online & other garden stores and will come with instructions on how & when to use. Some are liquids which can be watered in giving immediately accessible nutrients. Others are pellets or granules which need to be spread on the soil and release nutrients more slowly.

Now, onto the good bit - which delicious summer fruits and vegetables to choose? My top ten suggestions for a good range of versatile, mouth-watering produce are:

1. SALAD LEAVES: again a huge variety of salad leaves is available these days, from mustard leaves & Mizuna to wild rocket, spinach, lambs lettuce & chard. The great thing about these leaves is that they can grow relatively quickly and you can pick them as you need them. The ultimate 'cut & come again' summer vegetable! To make sure you have leaves available all summer, try starting seeds off on a window sill in February or March so that you can put them out early in the season. If you sow a few seeds at a time every other week, the leaves will be ready in succession rather than all at once. Don't worry too much about spacing them out in the pot - the leaves will happily grow quite densely as long as you are careful not to include proper lettuces which form a 'head' or ball.

2. STRAWBERRIES: well what can I say - can you imagine summer without strawberries? For me the smell of ripe strawberries is the essence of summer, reminiscent of hot days, sunshine, picnics & new mown grass. Wonderful! Even more wonderful is the fact that some thoughtful person has designed a container especially to allow lots of strawberries to be grown in a small space! The design of the pot means that it grows the strawberries in vertical layers so even a fairly small diameter pot may be able to take 10 -20 plants. Strawberry pots come in different sizes & materials (mine is terracotta) so they can be decorative as well as functional. But remember, the idea is to grow as many strawberries as possible - any excess makes great jam or dessert sauce (which can be frozen for later in the year). So look for pots that are double skinned to help warm up the compost & get your plants going. It is advisable to cover the pots with netting too otherwise birds & slugs will be enjoying your strawberries rather than you.

3. DWARF BEANS & PEAS: broad, French or runner beans & peas; all will do well in pots if you choose dwarf varieties. If your patio or growing area is in a windy spot you may need to stake your plants to prevent them from being damaged. A good early dwarf pea variety is Feltham First which can be sown the previous autumn, in a protected spot, where space allows.

4. COURGETTES (Zucchini): you will need quite a large pot for a courgette as they can spread out quite wide. Like the tomatoes, they will need lots of water and feeding to make sure of a bumper crop and prefer a warm spot on the patio. Pick the fruits while they are still small, that way the plant is stimulated to produce more and you are more likely to get them before the slugs do. The flowers are also considered to be a delicacy and can be stuffed & fried. Worth a try if you are feeling adventurous.

5. BEAUTIFUL BERRIES: strawberries may be summer incarnate but let's not forget the other mouth-watering soft fruits. It is perfectly possible to grow gooseberries, blackcurrants, blueberries & white & redcurrants in pots too. The size of the pot can be important here - there should be enough room for the plant's root system plus a small amount of room for expansion but more space than that will probably not achieve good results. That is good news for those with limited space or resources! It is better to re-pot soft fruit plants into a slightly larger container every year or two years (depending on size) than use an over large pot to start off with. The other main requirement is plenty of water! Juicy berries need water & sun to develop & ripen, they will also benefit from regular feeding.

Anyone wanting to grow blueberries or bilberries will need to use ericaceous compost rather than the usual sort. This is because, like heathers & many conifers, bilberries & blueberries need acidic soil. They need a mulch, to stop water loss from the soil and special feed to keep their soil acidic. Organic gardeners can use pelleted chicken manure but this is alkaline and so may need to be supplemented with some form of potash (mainly non-organic!). There are very few sources of organic potash although wood ash can be effective.

6. SWEET PEPPERS: colourful & tasty, peppers are easy to grow in pots. They germinate easily in small, plastic covered pots, on your window sill, and will grow to around 30cm. At this height the growing tips need to be pinched out to encourage new branches to grow. Keep potting up as the plants grow; they will probably need a 5 litre pot once they are ready to be put outside and a stake for support. If you have a wall to grow plants against, peppers will benefit from the warmth & reflected heat as will tomatoes & aubergines. Pepper Marconi Rosso is a good variety to try.

7. AUBERGINES (Eggplant): like the sweet peppers, aubergines make very colourful & attractive patio plants. They are grown in the same way as peppers and respond equally well to warmth. For an unusual variety, try aubergine Mohican which has white rather than purple fruits & is compact, only growing to around 60cm.

8. LEEKS: lovely, fresh & tangy either served raw & finely chopped in a salad or soft & melting under a coat of béchamel sauce. Leeks are easy to grow & can be densely planted in pots for picking while still young. That way you get lots of tender baby leeks rather than the big, tougher skinned more mature specimens.

So there we have it, just a few of the huge range of fruit and vegetables suitable for container growing. Remember, if it grows in soil it can probably be grown in a pot as long as the climatic conditions are right. So why not try growing some of your favourites in containers and see what happens - you may be pleasantly surprised.

Herbs

Planning an herb garden can be fun and rewarding. Herbs have been in use for centuries for culinary, medicinal and aromatic reasons. For generations tribal leaders and healers passed down the herbal secrets. Many modern medicines have an herb base. Modern herbalist mix medicinal herb for their clients. Many herbalists also mix aromatic herbs for beauty purposes. But, of course, the culinary herb is still the most widely used. You can become a kitchen gardener by growing an herb garden right in your kitchen on a sunny windowsill.

For the discussion of herbal gardening today we will plant the herbs found in the Elizabethan Era and so often mentioned in William Shakespeare's works. The plants selected will be culinary herbs, medicinal herbs and aromatic herbs, all to experience the aromas and flavours of that time.

Herbal gardening is wonderful since the herbs can be grown in a variety of ways. Plant a container garden for you deck or patio for great colours, different textures and super aromas. Planning an herb garden in the ground will allow you to cultivate a traditional kitchen herb garden outside. Or if you have limited space, become an inside kitchen gardener and plant your herbs on a windowsill or in a window box.

When planning your herb garden remember that the herbs need well drained soil, they hate wet feet. Test your soil for the herb garden and make sure it is alkaline. All Herbs need at least six hours of sunlight.

Here are the most common herbs found in an Italian herb garden: basil, bay, fennel, oregano, parsley, rosemary, sage, thyme, garlic etc. They are used in a variety of Italian recipes as well as other cuisines. These herbs are easy to grow, which makes it the herb garden for beginners and will give you a great sense of fulfilment when you use your herbs.

1. BASIL: refers to sweet Basil and all of the different varieties of Basil, and is used frequently because of its strong flavour. Its fragrance is a main stay of any Italian herb Garden. Basil is also a good companion plant and insect repellent. This herb can be over powering, start off by adding a little at a time to your dishes. This is an annual herb, which will need to be planted every year. In warm climates it will self-seed.

2. BAY LEAVES: Bay is easy to grow in an Italian herb garden; however there are many poisonous plants that look like Bay. You'll want to check with your local county extension office or the nursery expert to find out what the correct specie is for your area. The essential oils are in the leaves and the flavour is best after the leaves have been dried. When used in cooking the leaves are put in whole and then removed when the dish is finished.

3. FENNEL: No Italian herb garden should be without this herb, and it can be used in so many different ways. Almost every part of the plant can be used; the bulbs, seeds, and the leaves are used in a variety of different dishes. Fennel seeds are a common ingredient in Italian sausage. Sweet Fennel is often used for its seeds and fronds, the Florence variety for the stalks and bulbs. It has a liquorice flavour, and can be eaten raw, with some olive oil, lemon wedges and a little salt, as well as put into antipastos. While it is a perennial evergreen plant, it does need some protection in the winter, and it should be replanted ever few years, because it will start to lose its flavour. If you have some dill planted, it should be well away from Sweet Fennel, because it will cross-pollinate.

4. OREGANO: This is another common and popular herb that is included in every Italian herb garden. Oregano is used mainly in culinary dishes, but is also used for decoration, as well as medicinal purposes. There are two different kinds of Oregano: Mexican, and Greek. Oregano and Basil often are combined in many different sauces including pizza sauce, and marinades. It adds a special flavor to Italian cooking.

5. PARSLEY: there are many different varieties of parsley; you'll want Italian Parsley for your herb garden. It differs from the garnish variety due to its broad leaf. It is quite easy to grow in your Italian herb garden, and will re-seed itself it you let it go to seed. Parsley is another herb that can be added to just about every dish. Unfortunately slugs also love Parsley so take precautions against them.

6. ROSEMARY: Make room for Rosemary in your Italian herb garden. It can be used in just about any dish, and has been used for medicinal purposes for thousands of years as well as ornamental. Rosemary can be used fresh or dried; it has a very distinctive flavour. It is an evergreen shrub, is quite aromatic, and will attract bees to your garden. It is a perennial evergreen and can be harmed by frost; caution should be taken to protect it when the weather is extremely cold. Cut it back every spring to promote new growth.

7. SAGE: This is an evergreen bush that grows wild in many areas, and can be grown in your garden easily. In order to prevent Sage from getting unruly, you should keep it pruned back. It provides Italian food with a distinct flavour, including pork, and antipastos, as well as poultry. Sage wasn't as popular for a while, however it is still an important part of Italian cooking and with the new varieties it's regaining its popularity in the kitchen.

8. THYME: This herb has been used for centuries, not only as an additive in culinary dishes, but also in the bath water, and other medicinal purposes. Thyme is the herb to use in a dish when you are uncertain of what to use. If you are growing this versatile herb to cook with, make sure you are using Thymus Vulgaris, or common Thyme. It is quite easy to grow in your Italian herb garden, but this perennial tends to get quite woody after a few years and should be replaced about every two or three years.

9. GARLIC: Last, but certainly not least, herb gardening for beginners should always include Garlic, especially if you don't want to get smacked by your Italian relatives. Even though it may be called the 'stinking rose' by some, it is a very important herb, not only in cooking, but for its medicinal qualities. Eating a lot of garlic will keep you system detoxified. If you want your relatives to love you forever, use garlic in your dishes. It really doesn't matter what variety of garlic you grow, and it is easy to add to your garden.

10. Mint: With literally thousands of varieties of mint plants, you certainly have a broad choice for these very useful herb garden plants. Mint is incredibly easy to grow, but this can also be a problem because it can take over large areas of your outdoor garden because it grows and spreads so successfully and rapidly. I always recommend keeping mint plants in check by growing them strictly indoors in pots and containers.

11. CILANTRO AND CORIANDER (SEEDS): The cilantro plant is an annual, but with regular indoor planting throughout the year, you will always have cilantro growing and available. The entire cilantro plant is edible. Roots, stems, leaves and flowers, making the cilantro herb one of the most versatile and varied of your herb garden plants. Planting this vegetable needs a wider space since they spread their vines wide enough to cover the entire space. You should reserve an 18 inches distance between plants to prevent overcrowding as the plant progresses.

12. LETTUCE: This plant is the favourite by most house wives and vegetable lovers because of its nutritious and tender fresh leaves eaten as raw or mix with other vegetables as salads.
Lettuce is an easy to grow leafy vegetable and can thrives best either in shade location or open field. If you grow them in shade, at least they could get at least 3 -4 hours sunlight a day.

PART IV: TOOLS AND TECHNIQUES.

There are tools and tecniques that you should keep in mind and plan for, depending on the purpose of your land. Its size, financial considerations and various other factors should be taken into account.

Some of the important ones that should be considered while starting a farm are:

Planting Guides and Seeders

With all the plants available on the market these days, both from garden centres and mail order, you might wonder why anyone would bother to grow from seed. There are a few answers to this one but some of the basic ones are:

Personal satisfaction – there's nothing quite like seeing a garden full of plants that you grew yourself from a tiny seed.

Cost – if you have a large garden and want it full of bright flowers for the summer then the cheapest way is to grow your own bedding plants.

Choice – garden centres are great but in reality, they can't stock a fraction of the varieties available from specialist nurseries.

So if you fancy giving it a try, even if only in a small way, then this is what you will need to get started with seeds that need propagation indoors before planting out:

Seed trays, pots (or old margarine tubs, if you like, but trays are best). If you have a greenhouse or potting shed then those with drainage holes in the bottom are fine but if you're propagating your seeds on a windowsill then you'll be better off with the sort without drainage holes.

Seed tray covers. These aren't strictly necessary but they do help to keep warmth and moisture in during the propagation period and it saves messing around with plastic bags or film.

Potting compost. Do buy compost especially for seeds. All purpose compost is inclined to be a bit coarse for really tiny seeds.

Somewhere fairly constantly warm for germination (around 70°F, 20°C). If you want to grow your seeds in a greenhouse, you may need to consider heating it. Otherwise, an indoor windowsill should be alright or if you don't think that yours is warm enough, you can buy heated propagators or heated mats to put underneath seed trays.

Labels to stick on or in each pot or tray so that you know what's in it. Before you even open the seed packets, check the instructions. Some seeds need to be soaked, frozen or treated in some other way before use.

In general, one seed tray will accommodate one packet of seeds. Some, more specialised seeds come in much smaller quantities and a half size tray or a pot will be adequate.

Fill your container with compost to within about ¼ inch from the top then dampen it. I find that a spray bottle is ideal for this. You don't want the compost absolutely soaking wet or your seeds will rot. Either sprinkle the seeds all over the surface of your compost or make drills one inch apart with a pencil or your finger and sprinkle the seeds evenly into these. For larger seeds, you may need to make a small hole and drop each seed in individually. According to the instructions, either cover your seeds gently with more compost or leave exposed.

Dampen your compost again with the spray or a very fine trickle of water and unless it says otherwise on the packet, make some sort of mini greenhouse for your container. You can put plastic film over the top or put the whole tray into a clear plastic bag. For pots, you can slip a plastic bag over the top and hold in place with elastic bands.

Put your trays etc. in the aforesaid warm place, but not in direct sunlight, and wait for your seeds to grow. Depending on what they are, this could be days or weeks - it will usually tell you on the packet. In the meantime, check daily for sufficient water. If the plastic covering has water droplets inside you can be fairly sure that your compost is moist enough. If in doubt, feel gently with your finger. The soil should be damp, not wet!

When your seedlings start to appear and have grown a very tiny bit (not much more than ¼ inch), remove the plastic covering. From this point on, you will need to be even more vigilant that your trays don't dry out. I still advocate using the spray bottle for watering tiny seedlings - but be very careful, they will be fragile. If you are using draining trays or peat trays, you can water from the bottom if you prefer.

When your seedlings have developed 4 or 6 leaves and look a bit sturdier, you must thin them out to about one inch apart, in trays or pots. Prepare fresh trays or pots of compost - the next one on from seed compost. Separate the seedlings, using the tip of a pencil or the handle of a teaspoon to loosen them from the tray or pot. You must treat them with the utmost care as they are easily damaged at this stage. Gently tease the roots apart and try to only hold the leaves rather than the stems. Make holes in your newly-prepared compost and pop each seedling into a hole, gently firming down the soil around them. Some seedlings react very badly to transplanting and may look as though they are dying. Fear not, after a day or so, if they are kept moist and out of direct sunlight, they will be fine.

The new plants can now stay in these trays or pots until you are ready to put them into the ground or their outdoor containers. Keep them moist and give a little liquid feed at weekly intervals. If the plants look as though they are getting leggy, they don't have enough light and must be moved.

Seed planting is usually done early in the year (check packet for details). When the plants look quite sturdy and the weather has warmed up in spring, you can put your plants outside during the day to "harden" off. Make sure they are sheltered from heavy rain or wind. While the nights are still cold or there is a danger of frost, you will need to bring the plants in at the end of the day. Make sure that slugs and snails can't reach your new babies - a hungry slug can eliminate all your hard work at a sitting.

When all danger of frost has passed, you can put your plants in their permanent homes in your garden.

If you don't fancy all that fiddling around, there are a number of plants which can be sown from seed direct into the garden. To do this, make sure that the soil is a fine tilthe, sow your seeds in rows or clumps and cover with a little soil. Water sparingly and when they have germinated and grown on a little, thin them out to whatever distance apart it says on the packet by discarding the weakest looking seedlings.

Whichever method you choose, you should have a lovely bright garden for the summer.

Heated Water Platform

Chickens, as a rule, are pretty winter hardy animals. They can withstand some pretty cold temperatures (they're covered with feathers, after all) if they have a sheltered, draft-free place to live. One of the biggest concerns for your backyard flock is keeping their water fresh and unfrozen in the cold winter months.

To keep your chicken waterer from freezing, it helps to have an insulated, draft-free chicken coop in which to put the waterer. Many people also use a light bulb or timed heat lamp to add warmth to the inside of the coop. However, in really cold weather, those measures aren't enough to keep the water from freezing.

One simple solution to frozen water is to use a heated dog bowl. This is an especially useful solution for the small backyard chicken farmer. It's also a very affordable option, as many heated pet bowls are around $20 or so.

Another solution is to use a light bulb fountain heater. Essentially, this is a base with a lightbulb inside, and a platform that fits over the top. Your chicken waterer sits on top of the platform and the heat from the lightbulb keeps the water from freezing. In order to use this option, you need a metal waterer. This solution would run you around $50-70, but would allow you to water more chickens at one time, if you have a larger flock.

A third solution is to install a heater and thermostat in your chicken coop. Set it at 35 degrees. If the weather dips below 35, the heat will turn on, keeping your coop (and therefore your chicken waterer) above freezing.

If none of these ideas appeal to you, you can always do it the old-fashioned way and haul warm water out to your chicken coop several times a day, thaw out the chicken waterer and re-fill it with warm water. If that sounds like a crazy solution, just remember that you have it easier than your ancestors who would first have to build a fire and heat the water before hauling it out to the coop!

Regardless of the system you choose, remember that it's important to keep your chickens hydrated, even in the cold weather. Making sure they have fresh water will help your chickens stay healthy and, possibly, even laying eggs in the winter.

Support Your Plants.

Staking plants for support is important for vegetables and flowers. Large flowers often become top-heavy after a rain, so staking is a simple technique to keep them from sagging. Tall and delicately stemmed plants often require some support - especially during foul weather. Staking vegetable plants is an effective way to ensure a bountiful harvest.

Stakes are often forsaken at the expense of the flowers. Traditionally thought to be intrusive and unattractive, stakes, if used properly, are just the opposite. A carefully staked plant will show no visible support because the healthy and attractive foliage will hide the stakes or various strings and wires.

The best way to stake is to begin early in the growing season so you can easily train the plant and its foliage to cover whatever support system you have chosen. Staking mature plants whose foliage is flopping is a far more difficult task, and the leaves and flowers are not as appealing as if the plant were trained from the start. Even so, the health of a plant or flower is often necessary with late-maturity staking methods.

A stake should be planted about six inches shorter than your plant is likely to be at maturity. The stalk of the flower or vegetable should be firmly tied to the stake, but with enough slack to allow some movement for winds and growth.

Twine makes for an adequate tie, but strips of fabric may also be used, as can common, green garden plastic, cut into ½ inch wide strips that stretch.

If your garden has flowers needing support, a stake system can be situated to support the clump rather than each individual stalk or plant. Place stakes around the clump, then circle and criss-cross through the centre with your twine. For a nearly invisible look, you can use twigs and fishing line.

Bamboo stakes are quite common and can be purchased as thin as a pencil or up to a half inch or more in thickness, depending on how much support the plant requires. Round or square wire cages are sometimes used offering structural support for tomato plants. With cage-like structures, plants don't need to be tied, because the plant will grow through the wire and find its own support. These must be installed while the plant is quite young to be most effective. Wire rings may also be purchased at local garden centres for similar purpose.

Other plants like climbers and vines may thrive as ground cover, but will grow to create a wonderful dimension of height in your garden. Usually, any type of support structure will do for these purposes, as long as the plant can grow through and around it. Trellises are the most commonly used support structures, but you can be creative and use a flea market find - even a section of lattice fencing or stretch of chicken wire

Staking plants for support is important for vegetables and flowers. Traditionally thought to be intrusive and unattractive, stakes, if used properly, are just the opposite round or square wire cages are sometimes used for offering structural support for tomato plants. Trellises are also a commonly used support structures. Even a section of lattice fencing or stretch of chicken wire can be used to support plants. Twine is a commonly used item to secure plants to a support.

Winning the Battle of the Weeds.

Weeds are generally perennial or annual in nature and they grow from seeds. They are unwanted plants or grasses that can damage your beloved plants. Weeds occupy space and utilize nutrients from the soil that are meant for the plants. Growth of lots weeds can impact the overall appearance of your garden and it is important to get rid of them effectively so that they do not re- appear to cause harm to your plants.

There are many types of weeds that can emerge in your garden and it is crucial to identify them so that you can take necessary steps to remove them. Weeds can be broadly classified into two types which are Grass Weeds and Broad Leaf Weeds. As the name suggests, grass weeds are thin and grass like in appearance and the other ones have broad leaves. Some of the common weeds that can be found in gardens are Annual Bluegrass, Foxtails, Nettles, Dandelions, Bindweed, Twitch Grass, Horsetail, Goosegrass, Crabgrass and Carpetweed.

There are several physical and chemical methods of getting rid of the weeds from the garden. Non- chemical ways of removing weeds are generally preferred by the home gardeners as they do not want to use toxic chemicals and herbicides in the garden. Some of the common methods that can help you to control the abnormal growth of weeds in your garden are-

Cultivation – Cultivation is the most common method which is used extensively in home gardens. Farms and fields are cultivated with the help of big tractor mounted cultivators. Home gardeners can use hoe to get rid of the weeds from soil level. While hoeing, make sure that you do not go deeper as it might bring the buried seeds closer to the germination area.

Hand Pulling – Hand pulling is probably the easiest way of removing weeds if they have not spread and covered a large area. You can occasionally remove the weeds by hand whenever you come across one while strolling in the garden. This way the flower beds will be clean and free from weeds. However, hand pulling is not feasible if the weed growth is quite high and you will have to rely on alternate methods to get rid of them.

Mulching – Mulching is an effective way of keeping the weeds away from the plants. Mulch cover on the soil does not let the weeds to germinate and grow easily. Mulching can noticeably reduce the growth of unnecessary weeds in your garden.

Herbicides – Herbicides are chemical in nature and they can be sprayed to kill the weeds. Herbicides can kill the weeds in germination stage and they can also destroy pre existing mature weeds. However, it is advisable not to use herbicides in the home gardens as they can also cause damage to some of the plants.

Fumigants – Fumigants are also chemical in nature and they kill all the living creatures in the soil like weeds, seeds, insects and disease carrying organisms.

Groundcovers – Cover crops or ground cover plants are also beneficial in controlling weeds. Groundcover plants spread on the ground and they do not allow the weeds to grow.

These are some of the methods that can help you in getting rid of weeds from your home garden. It is important to realize the fact that you cannot get rid of them completely as they will emerge again over a period of time. However, you can control them effectively so that they do not spread in the entire garden.

PART V: GREATER FOOD SELF-SUFFICIENCY.

As we watch food prices continue to climb, with many signs supporting continued escalation, healthy home made foods are might become a financial challenge. We need to eat to live, and we need to eat well to thrive, so we don't have much of a choice but to let the grocery stores hit our wallets hard...or do we? Home food gardens are an excellent way to enjoy healthy produce without paying a premium for it, and becoming self sufficient has enriching benefits for one's personal sense of well-being, as well. Once you prepare a garden, it will continue to produce food throughout the season - save the seeds each harvest and you'll have a perpetual food source!

Home food gardens can be placed almost anywhere, with traditional gardens in the backyard, box gardens, indoor verticle gardems or community gardens in apartment style housing complexes. Very easy to set up, materials like tomato cages or bean trellises can be reused season after season, and provided the soil is well-aerated, fertilized, and turned over before planting each year, it can also be counted on to produce delicious food to help you become more financially secure and less reliant on the industrial food complex. The truly savvy gardener embraces self sufficient living by composting his or her produce scraps as well - these will break down into nutrient-rich soil that will lead to bigger, healthier plants and a greater yield.

If you'd rather keep your money in your pocket or have it grow in other investments, than spending it at the grocery store, you can ensure your success at self sufficient living by doing a little research before beginning your garden. Check to see what plants grow best in your region and area, making these the heart of your garden. Don't neglect planting a few herbs as well - these will give flavor to your produce and make them savory and delicious! When you grow your own food, you can control what goes into it and you don't have to worry about unknown pesticides and chemical additives. In addition, you save the gas that you'd use to go to the grocery store so often, which is great for your budget and better for the planet overall.

While becoming self sufficient and financially secure with a food garden sounds appealing, some may be skeptical it is too much work or effort. With modern technology, this is never a worry! Products like soaker hoses, watering bulbs, and slow-release fertilizer spikes practically do the work for you, ensuring you don't have to lug around a heavy watering can, or risk losing your fruit and vegetables to nutrient deficiency.

A food garden is not only economical and easy to set up and use, it is also a beautiful addition to your property and a great use of space. When you weigh the price of pounds of your favorite organic produce against the very small price of a packet containing hundreds of seeds, the choice is an easy one:

Making Your Own Country Wines.

Wine making at home is not tough at all and it is actually a very cool hobby.

You can make wine from home one of two ways. One is from a kit that comes with instructions and is usually made with something along the lines of grape concentrate. The other way is to do it from scratch step-by-step. This way is much more rewarding. And although making wine from home from scratch, step-by-step, is more time-consuming and more difficult the results are much better as you have total control of the type of wine you make, how it tastes, and the quality of the wine overall. If you are looking to make wine cheaply and quickly and are not too concerned about quality then a wine making kit will suffice. If you want to make a wine that you can be glowing with pride from then read on.

You can make wine successfully from many different types of fruits not only the obvious grapes but also apricots, plums, elderberries, pears, peaches, apples. You can pretty much make your own wine from home using almost any fruit.

Here is a list of the equipment and supplies you will need to make your very own fine wine.
• A large plastic tub where steel pot to press juice into. A lid will be required.
• Something to squeeze or press the fruit with. The easiest way is to use an electric juicer.
• A glass vessel that will be used to ferment and store the fruit juice such as a jug. You can get the proper vessel at a brewing shop or online at a wine making supply website.
• A plastic tube for siphoning purposes.
• Yeast which is available at your local super market
• Sugar
• You will also need something to clean your equipment. You can either use boiling water or sterilizing solutions or tablets.

Step one to making your own wine at home – get your juice
Press the fruit you are going to use to make your home wine either using a hand press or the electric juicer. You will want enough juice to fill the glass fermentation vessels you are using.

A lot of times a wine making recipe will recommend watering down your juice to get the volume you need. If you want the absolute best results do not do this as this will cut down on the flavour of the end product.

Do not be afraid to get creative. There is nothing wrong with mixing the juice from several different types of fruits together to make your own unique blend of wine. In the beginning if you are new to making wine from home you may not want to wing it like this. You can follow a step-by-step recipe.

Many sources of juice exist, and most of them can be found no matter where you live:

Table grapes bought at the store: these will usually lack ripeness. This can be overcome either by adding sugar in the juice, or by letting them ripe and desiccate somewhat in a dry and temperate place. This will increase their sugar concentration naturally but also their flavour (this is a traditional technique used in various regions of Europe to make sweet wines).

Grape concentrates: these are usually sold with wine kits. This is probably the most convenient way to get your juice, but probably not the best one in terms of quality. Unfortunately, the process of concentration often alters the flavour and the aromatics. However, it can be a great way to get started.

Packaged juices: this is a convenient solution and allows making wine from any fruit or combination of fruits. Results can be great too, if you use only high-quality juice, made from whole, fully ripe fruits. It is also important to use juices without any preservative added, as these will prevent fermentation.

For the ones who have the chance to live in a viticultural area: Vitis Vinifera fresh grapes (a species of European grape specially used for winemaking) are clearly the "gold standard" of winemaking. However, this is also the most difficult path, requiring more equipment and work. But the results can be stunning - or awful if something goes wrong. Definitely the solution for the highly passionate!

Frozen grapes: some grape producers sell these for amateur winemakers. The freezing process keeps intact all the qualities of the grapes, so this is a great choice. However this solution has nearly the same drawbacks as the fresh grapes solution.

And of course, you can also use fresh fruits, in the same way as fresh grapes.

Whatever your final choice, you should take care of three crucial factors if you want to get great results. First, ripeness, which is essential if you want to get full-bodied, rich wines. Then, quality: no excess fertilizers, chemicals or irrigation during the growing process. Whenever possible, choose good-tasting varieties grown under the right climate. This will bring complexity and more flavour to your wine. And finally, be careful about sanitary state: any trace of decay must be avoided on fresh fruits. In addition to bringing some bad flavour, decay is also a real problem for fermentation.

Step two to making your own wine from home – add the sugar
Very sweet juices will not need the addition of sugar to the recipe. The main purpose of the sugar is that of fermentation or the production of alcohol. Fruits that are naturally very sweet like a sweet grapes will not need the addition of sugar. If you decide to add sugar generally speaking add anywhere between 1 - 2 pounds of sugar per 1 gallon of fruit juice or lesser amount if you want a drier wine.

One thing you can do if you like to experiment is make several different batches of the same wine varying the amount of sugar that you use in each batch so if you have a five glass vessels for example you can use a slightly different amount of sugar for each vessel making note of the results of the end product. You can also use the same experimentation process to experiment with different fruits and fruit combinations. With time and experience you will be able to develop your own unique fine wine that no one else has. Keep in mind the more sugar you use the higher the alcohol content will be of the wine when you are finished.

Add the sugar to the fruit juice by warming the fruit juice and a pot stirring in the sugar. Warming the fruit juice first will ensure the sugar gets dissolved completely.

Step number three to making wine from home – add the yeast

Make sure your glass vessels are sterilized with the sterilizing solution or tablets or boiling water. Put the sugar fruit juice into the glass vessel. Add the powdered yeast and a little warm water and sugar into a cup to dissolve it. Leave it for a few minutes. This will start the activation process of the yeast. Add the yeast to the fruit juice mixture. Put your airtight lid on top. The yeast will convert the sugar into alcohol as your wine ferments.

The fermentation process is what distinguishes wine from grape juice. In order for the fermentation process to work, wine yeast is needed.

The Importance of Wine Yeast

The most important ingredient in wine making is wine yeast. It is not only an important ingredient but the process of mixing it with the must can make or break the wine. The yeast works by absorbing the sugar from the fruit and turning it into both alcohol and carbon dioxide.

Buying Wine Yeast

The process of buying wine yeast is a fairly uncomplicated one. Make sure that the label reads something to effect of wine making yeast. Generic brands work well as do the specialty brands that the wine making connoisseurs may be using. A little wine making yeast goes a long way so be aware that a 10 milligram packet of yeast mixes with 10 gallons of must.

Activating the Yeast

The yeast must be activated before it is mixed into the must. This process will ensure that optimum results are received once the two are mixed together. To activate the yeast, mix it with a cup of juice squeezed from the must and set aside for at least 12 hours before mixing it into the must. If you happen to forget to set aside a cup of juice from the must, using a cup of lukewarm water in it's place will work just as well. Once the yeast is activated, it will appear as it is boiling.

Timing
The timing of mixing in the yeast with the must is crucial. It is of utmost importance to not mix it in too early or too late. Wine yeast is mixed in with the must at least 24 hours after the fruit has been crushed. It then begins the fermentation process and continues for 5 to 7 days and should be stirred no more than 2-3 times per day.

While the hardest part of wine making is the wine yeast process, it is a relatively simple one once you know what to buy, how to use it, when to mix it and why it is a crucial part of the whole wine making process. Now you have no excuse not to make yourself a batch of delicious homemade wine.

Step number four to making your own homemade wine – the most important step, patience

Put your fermentation vessels (the glass jugs with the sugar wine yeast mixture) in a warm place generally speaking between 70 and 85°F. For the best results you want to let your wine ferment for at least six months. For best results up to a year. If you are inpatient and drink your wine too soon you will not be satisfied with the results.

For many people this waiting part is the toughest part as they are anxious to drink their own homemade wine.

As your wine mixture ferments you will notice the accumulation of dead yeast cells on the bottom of the glass jug. Leaving this dead yeast in the wine mixture will affect the taste quality negatively. The way to combat this is about once a month or so siphon the wine out into a new glass vessel making sure not to siphon the dead yeast from the bottom of the original glass vessels.

Check on your wine every couple weeks. Depending upon how much this dead yeast is accumulating you may want to siphon the wine a little more or less frequently than once a month.

By definition only those beverages which are obtained through fermentation of grapes are called wines. Those which are produced from rice or starchy raw materials are called rice wine, sake or barley wine. Those wines which are produced from any other thing are called fruit wines.

The pros and cons of chemicals in fermentation process

Fermentation was used in ancient times to prevent food from getting spoiled. Today, it is better known for the addition of alcohol than anything else. The alcohol percentage in the wine is due to the fermentation started and supported by the sugar. In order to prevent the growth of the toxic organisms, the modern world adds sulphur dioxide to the wine. The advantages of this additive are that it is an excellent anti-oxidant which can totally stabilize the wine fermentation and prevent damage.

However, the disadvantages of this added chemical is found in the possibility of triggering acute allergies in people who consume the wine. Other symptoms are nausea, vomiting, headache and even the triggering of asthma. Since, all the above symptoms are very serious, the adding of chemicals to stabilize the fermentation process has been reduced and even banned in some places.

The pros and cons of natural fermentation

Most people all over the world will always prefer one hundred per cent natural way of fermentation of the wine. Most of the time, it is indeed that greatest gift from Gods. However, there are times when uncontrolled growth of microbes influence the process of fermentation and alter the taste, color and texture of the wine, completely ruining it.

While searching for natural ways to stop wine for spoilage researchers have found lactic acid bateria, also known as LAB as one of the most promising types of bacteria that can fight against the harmful micro-organisms quite effectively and hence, protect the wine from any further damage. Since it is natural, it is accepted happily by all the organic enthusiasts all over the world.

There is only one concern - these types of bacteria do not act on gram-negative bacteria, for example moulds and yeasts. Hence, if these are present and you consume the wine, you will fall sick. However, if you measure the odds, it will be very rare that they reach to such an extent.

The conclusion
Both the processes are useful in their own way. However, since the world is moving away from chemicals and their usage in food, it is far more preferable to use the natural way to start fermentation, and the stop it.

The main concerns in using either of the systems for fermentations and controlling the bacterial growth, is public safety. If safety is assured, then everything will be perfect. This will also assure higher quality, and will demand a higher price as well. Once the natural preservatives (in the form of friendly bacteriocins) then the Sulphur dioxide can be reduced or even eliminated from the wine production, other than using it in a very limited condition as an anti-oxidant.

The final step to making wine from home – bottling your wine
Place the wine in a cold place for one to two weeks however make sure you do not freeze it. Generally speaking a temperature of between 40 to 50°F. is good. This will improve the wines clarity making it a better quality. Bottle the wine and cork it. There are places you can go online to get your own custom wine labels.

If you are serious about wine making as you are making wine you want to keep accurate records of the exact techniques, ingredients, and methods you use to make each batch of wine. This way when you make a superb batch of wine you will have the exact recipe for that and you can replicate it for years to come.

If you are really fanatical about the quality of your wine let your wine sits on a rack for a couple of years. At this point you are probably so excited about drinking your own homemade wine this may be difficult. What I would recommend you do is make a large enough batch so you can bottle and rack most of it for several years and still have enough left over to enjoy and drink now.

Easy Wine Recipes to Make at Home

I want to make my own wine and beer!

Wine and beer making may be as old as civilization but it still holds the same fascination for us today as I am sure it did for our ancestors over a thousand years ago. There is still something magical about the fermentation process that intrigues us. Wine and beer making is an entirely natural process that can and will happen without any human intervention. But over the years the human race has harnessed this natural phenomenon to produce some outstanding wines and beer. Maybe that's why it fascinates us so much. Wine and beer making can be enjoyed and perfected by anyone. I have been to wine competitions were homemade wines have put professional wine tasters in awe. Anybody can make outstanding beer and wine. You must remember that just about every great wine and beer maker started out just like you

Since beer and wine-making has been around forever it is only naturally that it is part of our folklore. There are many tall tales about the potency of homemade wine and beer and stories about the dangers of drinking homemade alcohol. Most of these stories are totally untrue and some are downright silly. Here is a list of some facts you might like to know.

Wine and beer-making is safe. Pathogenic bacteria (the stuff that makes you sick) cannot survive in wine or beer. The common spoilage bacterium that can survive in alcohol will make your wine or beer unpalatable but it will not harm you.

The alcohol made by the fermentation of sugar is ethyl alcohol and should not be confused with its deadly cousin Methyl (wood) alcohol. All of the stories you hear about people going blind and been poisoned was by the accidental consumption of methyl alcohol. I repeat this is not the type of alcohol you will be making.

You can make wine or beer that is as good or better than the commercial stuff. They make it just like you do at home, but only on a larger scale.

Most wine and beer contains 12 or 5 percent alcohol respectively and should remain that way if you wish to maintain the traditional characteristics of these beverages.

Fermented alcoholic beverages can reach a maximum of about 20% percent alcohol by volume (and that is with some difficulty). To reach higher alcohol levels you will have to distill which is illegal in most of North America.

Quality wine or beer is made by using the best ingredients. This is an area where amateurs often err. They think that if they buy some cheap malt or grape concentrate and their first wine or beer is a failure then they haven't lost much. Wrong. If you buy cheap malt or concentrate your chances of failure increase ten fold and you are most likely to be disappointed and give up the hobby. Don't make that mistake.

What do I need to get started?

Most people should consider a prepackaged equipment starter kit. These kits have all the basic equipment necessary to start wine and beer-making and they are usually sold at a discount. You can add all the extra gadgets as you go on. You will also need a wine or beer ingredient kit. Listed below are the essentials you will need to make your own wine and beer.

An equipment starter kit is a onetime purchase which you will use for all your future wine and beer-making. Here is an outline of what you will find in most starter kits.

A 25 - 30 litre (5.5 - 6.5 gallon) fermenting buckets with sealable lid drilled to accept an air lock.

An air lock and rubber stopper which creates a one-way valve that lets CO2 gas escape from the fermenting liquid but prevents oxygen from entering.

A long handle plastic stirring spoon which makes it easy to stir a 5 gallon bucket of liquid.

Thermometer

A glass or plastic carboy. (a large 5 gallon bottle similar to those you see on water coolers). Your wine or beer is transferred to this for bulk aging and clearing.

Siphoning tube and attachments used to transfer your wine between your fermenting bucket and carboy.

Sanitizing powder and instruction booklet.

Some start kits may also contain a hydrometer with sample jar and a crown capper or wine corker.

You got the equipment now you need the ingredients. We recommend that you purchase a wine or beer ingredient kit. These contain everything you need to make your wine or beer. All you need to do is add water and start the fermentation! Here is a list of what you can expect to find in a wine or beer ingredient kit.

Wine kits usually contain a blend of grape concentrate, grape juice and sugar. Premium kits such as our Cru Select are 100% grape product and have no added sugar. The kit will also contain a packet of yeast, a packet of stabilizer and a packet of finings or clarifier. Some kits may also contain oak chips and elderberries.

Beer kits will contain hopped malt extract and yeast. Most beer kits will also need the addition of 1 kilogram or 2 1/4 lb. of sugar. Premium kits such as our Brew House and Tundra have either the sugar added or use all-grain without added sugar.

Making Your Own Vinegar.

Making vinegar is easier than making wine or beer and requires minimal equipment or ingredients. Other than a vinegar crock and the wine or beer you'll be using, you can get everything else you need for under $30. Here are the items you'll need:

Vinegar Crock Vinegar can theoretically be made in any sort of container. Traditionally, it is made in oak barrels called vinegar casks or in ceramic urns known as vinegar crocks. There are three important features in a container used to make vinegar. The container should have a mouth wide enough that you can insert your vinegar raft and preferably your whole hand. It should have a tap, spout, or spigot near the bottom, but far enough from the bottom that it doesn't pick up sediment. Finally, it should be made of a material that will not react with the vinegar. Vinegar is a dilute acid, so it will react with most metals given time.

Given these features, you are not constrained to only use products officially sold as vinegar crocks. Anything officially sold as a vinegar crock will quite frankly be seriously over-priced. I looked on the Internet recently and found many of them priced at nearly $100!

I use two containers to make vinegar. One is a miniature ceramic water crock that holds a half gallon. It costs $24. The other is a one-gallon plastic beverage dispenser I picked up at a department store for $4. Both of these containers have the essential features, including the spigot. Normal ceramic water crocks hold 2½ gallons, an amount which may far exceed the amount of vinegar you plan to make. That's why I got a miniature ½ gallon crock.

You could go all out and get an oak vinegar cask, but that will set you back at least $80. If you want your vinegar to be oak-aged, just add oak cubes to the sealed pint or quart jar that you are using to age your vinegar.

Cheesecloth and Rubber Bands

These items are used over the mouth of your vinegar crock to allow oxygen to enter but keep fruit flies and other critters out. Not all cheesecloth is created equal. The material that is sold as "cheesecloth" at the supermarket is not suitable for making cheese, and even doubled or tripled it won't keep fruit flies out of your vinegar.

Unless you have a good gourmet shop nearby that sells real cheesecloth, you may have to order it from a supplier of cheese-making supplies over the Internet. It is a bit expensive when you include shipping, so I recommend saving on shipping by ordering a couple of packages. They won't go to waste because you'll need the cheesecloth for making cheese in the next chapter.

The size of the needed rubber bands will be different depending upon the size of the mouth of your vinegar crock. The only caution worth mentioning is that light and vinegar fumes will degrade the rubber, so check the rubber bands weekly and replace them if you see signs of deterioration. Otherwise you'll look at your crock one day and find more flies in it than vinegar.

Miscellaneous Supplies

A vinegar raft is a small thin piece of oak that floats on top of your vinegar. Its purpose is to keep the vinegar mother from sinking because if the vinegar mother sinks, it will stop making vinegar. These are available in vinegar kits or individually from many Internet sites. Just type "vinegar raft" into a search engine.

Some people prefer the taste of vinegar that has been aged in oak, or the astringency contributed by the tannins leached from the oak. Oak barrels are expensive and time-intensive to maintain. An alternative is adding oak chips or oak cubes to the vinegar. Add a quarter cup per gallon, enclosed in a tied spice bag for easy removal later. The chips or cubes are added during the aging process and left in the vinegar for four to six weeks. For these purposes, you don't want to use oak from your building supply store. Instead, order it from a winemaking supplier. Winemaking suppliers can offer a range of oaks with different taste characteristics that you know aren't contaminated with anything nasty.

Canning jars are a good choice for aging and storing vinegars. They seal tightly, which will cause the vinegar mother to go dormant during aging, and they can be used repeatedly which makes them a good bargain.

One other thing you may find helpful is a funnel that you have attached to a piece of plastic hose such as the hose used for racking wine. As vinegar is being made, you need to add more beer or wine. The easy way to do this without risk of disturbing the vinegar mother is to insert the hose into the liquid in the vinegar crock, and add the liquid through the funnel.

A candy thermometer will be needed for pasteurizing vinegar, unless you plan to can it using a boiling water bath canner for long-term storage.

Consolidated Equipment and Ingredient List
- Vinegar crock
- Vinegar mother
- Cheesecloth
- Rubber bands
- Vinegar raft
- Canning jars
- Candy thermometer
- Oak chips or cubes (optional)

Making Your Vinegar
The first thing to do is pre-dilute your wine or beer if needed. At levels higher than 7% alcohol it might inhibit the AAB. You can always make it less concentrated, down to 3%, for purely culinary use or if your beer only has that much alcohol and it isn't unusual for sherry vinegars to be as high as 7%. In general, I recommend diluting to 5.5% so the vinegar can be used with greater versatility. Always dilute with clean, non-chlorinated water. I use bottled water for this purpose.

So ... how much water do you add to your beer or wine to get a certain percentage of alcohol? Start by dividing the current concentration in percent by the desired concentration in percent to get C. So if I have some 10% wine and I want 5.5%, I divide 10 by 5.5 to get 1.82. Next, multiply the volume of your wine (say 500 ml in a standard wine bottle) by C to get the total diluted volume: 500ml × 1.82 = 910. Finally, subtract the volume of wine from the total volume to get the volume of water you need to add. 910 ml − 500 ml = 410 ml. This also works with beer. Say I have some beer that is 6% alcohol and I want to dilute it to 5.5%. The standard beer bottle is 12 ounces. So C = 6%/5.5% = 1.09. Multiply 12 oz × 1.09 = 13. Finally, 13 − 12 = 1, so I would add one ounce of water.

The quantity of diluted wine or beer that you use is important because it takes a while for the vinegar mother to work, and in the meantime the underlying beer or wine is vulnerable to outside infection. You want to limit the amount you put in the crock to no more than triple the volume of the vinegar mother, which is eight ounces. So your initial ingredients of the vinegar crock will be 24 ounces of beer or wine diluted as needed and eight ounces of vinegar mother for a total of 32 ounces.

Making Vinegar, Step by Step

1. Clean your vinegar crock thoroughly and sanitize it using sulphite solution. (See the chapters on wine for how to make sulphite solution.)
2. Check the capacity of the container of vinegar mother you ordered. Usually it is eight ounces.
3. Add diluted wine or beer to the vinegar crock. The amount added should be twice the volume of the vinegar mother. So if you have eight ounces of vinegar mother, put 24 ounces of wine or beer in your crock. The alcohol percentage cannot exceed 7%.
4. Open your vinegar mother. If it is gelatinous, place your vinegar raft on top of the water/wine solution in the vinegar crock.

5. Add the vinegar mother. If it is all liquid, just gently pour it into the crock. If it is gelatinous, add it on top of the vinegar raft.

6. Cover the mouth of the container with cheesecloth and hold it in place with a rubber band.

7. Set the container in a dark place or at least someplace well out of the sun. The ideal temperature range is 80 to 90 degrees, but it will progress fine at 70 to 100.

8. Depending on temperature and other factors, the complete conversion of wine to vinegar can take anywhere from six weeks to three months. Check your vinegar weekly by sniffing it through the cheesecloth. It should smell like vinegar is forming.

9. To increase the volume of the vinegar being made, you can add more diluted wine or beer starting at the fourth week and every fourth week thereafter. Add by using a sanitized funnel and tubing.

10. Six weeks after the final addition of wine, start tasting small (less than ¼ tsp) samples of the vinegar to see if it is done. It's done when the entire alcohol flavour has been replaced with vinegar flavour. Your tongue and nose are amazingly sensitive and able to detect many substances in very low concentrations of parts-per-million. This is as accurate as any easily performed test in determining if the vinegar is done.

11. Once the vinegar is done, it is important to remove it from the vinegar crock because with all the alcohol gone, the vinegar mother will start consuming the acetic acid, and thereby destroy the vinegar. Take out as much vinegar as you can through the spigot and then start your next batch using the same vinegar mother in that container. As long as your vinegar doesn't become contaminated, you can use the same vinegar mother indefinitely.

Making Cheese at Home.

Ask any group of people what their favourite comfort foods are and most likely cheese is involved. What if you could make you own cheese at home anytime you wanted and it would be ready that same day! That's what I did. I have always been into projects. For a long time I have made my own wine and vinegar. I also like to cook. One day while looking up recipes on the net I found a site for making homemade cheese. My curiosity was peaked. I could make my own brand of cheese to cook with or serve with my own wine! AWSOME!

I did some research on the web about homemade cheese and found all the resources I needed. Not only that, I found a one stop shop for over 700 different types of exotic cheeses. (I had a couple wheels shipped to my house) I also realized home cheese making, on a small scale, is much more art than science. You need a basic understanding of the science but in the end, your cheese will be your own. If you are new to cheese making, and wish to try this rewarding cottage craft you won't be disappointed. It is amazing how easy it is to make your own homemade cheese. A simple cream yogurt cheese spread can be ready for breakfast overnight. Homemade mozzarella cheese is ready the same day it's made. That's right; you can make mozzarella cheese in only one hour. Even the aged cheeses like Cheddar, Gouda and Colby are ready to eat in just a few weeks.

The basic ingredients for making homemade cheese are milk, starter culture and or natural acids, and rennet. (a milk-curdling enzyme) Cheese can be made from any dairy animal milk. First place the stock pot of milk on the stove over medium heat. It is important that you heat the milk slowly. Sprinkle in the citric acid and mild lipase powder while you gently stir. Heat slowly until the milk reaches 88 degrees. Stir every few minutes to prevent scorching the milk on the bottom of the pot. You will begin to see the curd develop. Once the milk reaches 88 degrees F. stir in the diluted calcium chloride then the rennet and water mixture. Continue stirring every few minutes until the milk reaches 105 degrees F. Turn off the heat and let the milk set covered for 15 minutes at 105 degrees. Curd (white mass) and whey (greenish liquid) will now be fully separated. Use a slotted spoon or strainer to transfer the curd to a dish. If the curd is too soft to transfer, let the milk sit a few more minutes. Pour off as much of the whey as you can. Gently press the curds together with the spoon and force more whey out of them. Squeeze out and drain as much whey as possible. At this point your soft cheese is done. You will end up with a creamy white cheese with a tender curd and a fresh, tangy flavour. You can throw this homemade cheese in the refrigerator for later, or enjoy it straight away.

To make a homemade cheese firmer just takes a little bit longer, and requires a couple more tools. Line a sieve or a basket with a double thickness of cheesecloth or a coarse, porous towel. First rinse in cold water, and set it over a bowl. Ladle the curds into the sieve and season them with salt, roughly a half-teaspoonful. The whey, which will drain into the bowl, can be used for baking. Great for bisquets. Refrigerate overnight or until the cheese is well drained. Tie the ends of the cheesecloth over a wooden spoon balanced over a bowl and let it hang until all the whey has drained out. Fold back the top layers of the cheesecloth or towelling and turn the cheese carefully out onto a plate. The imprint of the cloth will be left on the cheese. To make hard homemade cheese put the cheeses in a cheese press and let sit for several more hours.

There are many things that can be done with this cheese. It can be enjoyed by you, or served on a tray at a party, and let's not forget about cooking. Let's hope everyone reading this article is ready to ban the blue box from their kitchen, and is open to the magic of homemade cheese and macaroni. I can say from experience that I have never tasted something so fulfilling. Layers of my fresh homemade cheese piled over warm macaroni. It's like a favourite blanket. The three cheeses in Martha Stewart's recipe for Macaroni & cheese are White Cheddar, Havarti, and Muenster. All these you can make at home.

CONCLUSION.

Whether you're planning to start a small farm, begin organic farming, start a country Bed & Breakfast, or earn money from your garden, to begin making this dream come true, start with the concept of the "Mini Farm" that brings them all together. It's the 21st century version of sustainably producing from the land in larger quantities in smaller space than any time in history, because with technology and world travel, humans have now discovered and blended the best growing techniques that combine ancient discoveries (such as Chinese or French intensive growing methods) with cutting edge research on creating living soils and sustainable food supplies in smaller spaces than ever before understood.

To start a small farm, use micro eco-farming techniques to begin from as small as a half-acre, and even stop there, or grow into a few more acres if you have the land. Start in your spare time until your business has built up enough to let you quit your office job. Micro eco-farming involves organic farming techniques, but adds beyond organics to make your mini-farm more productive than any farm in humankind's history.

To start a country Bed & Breakfast, plan your B&B's breakfast menus first, and then design the small farm to grow the menu's products, the organic farm that will wrap around your B&B from the information gleaned from your menu. You may want to raise laying hens, blueberries, strawberries, a few antique apple and pear trees, an herbal tea garden, and a couple dairy goats. Your B&B customers will love this small farming demonstration and setting, and it all "synergizes." The goats and hens will provide organic fertilizer along with ingredients for breakfast omelets and yogurt, the chickens and goats can eat prunings from the plant crops, which will provide your customers with freshly baked blueberry muffins, strawberry jam and pear butter (which can also be sold as a product to your customers) and spicy apple bread and apple cider.

To make money from your garden, the possibilities are endless. You can grow a cutting garden with a flower stand out front to earn money from your garden, or sell the flower bouquets to in-town B&Bs that don't grow their own, or to restaurants and hotels; sell high priced rare gourmet food crops to nearby five star restaurants, such as rare edible flowers or fresh ethnic food crops.

Whether you plan to start a small farm, earn money in organic farming, make money from your garden, or open a country Bed & Breakfast, your livelihood will be helping restore the planet by maintaining green life and living soil to your outdoor "office."

Printed in Great Britain
by Amazon